CREATE YOUR APP AND GROW RICH!

How successful entrepreneurs across the world are creating world-class app businesses from an idea, and how you can do the same.

First published in 2017
Melbourne, Australia

© Appomate Pty Ltd 2017
The moral rights of the author have been asserted.
This book is a SpiritCast Network Book

National Library of Australia Cataloguing-in-Publication data:

Author:
        Krishnamoorthy, Barath
Title:
        Create Your App And Grow Rich
ISBN-13:
        978-1-387-01392-0

Editor-in-chief: Anita Saunders
Cover Design: Bliss Inventive

Disclaimer:
The material in this publication is of the nature of general comment only, and does not represent professional advice. It is not intended to provide specific guidance for particular circumstances and it should not be relied on as the basis for any decision to take action or not take action on any matter which it covers. Readers should obtain professional advice where appropriate, before making any such decision. To the maximum extent permitted by law, the author and publisher disclaim all responsibility and liability to any person, arising directly or indirectly from any person taking or not taking action based on the information in this publication.

DEDICATION

I dedicate this book, all the love and work that has gone into creating this, to people everywhere who truly care for a better world. I dedicate it to all the clients I have worked with in the last eight years, my mentors, my team in Australia and India, my beautiful friends and family who have helped me learn and grow. I dedicate this book to everyone who advocates for more fun and freedom in human life.

CONTENTS

INTRODUCTION FROM THE AUTHOR

There has never been a time when opportunities for growth were better. What once took 30 years to achieve is now being done in three years. Companies like Uber, Airbnb, and Facebook grew into multi-billion dollar enterprises within five to six years of launching, helping billions of people across the world. Such an achievement, unimaginable for traditional brick-and-mortar companies, can happen now thanks to the scalability of app businesses. This means any entrepreneur can impact millions or even billions of people positively with their idea. For the first time in history, we have millionaires still in their teens and billionaires in their twenties, not because they are much smarter than entrepreneurs of previous generations, but because of this very opportunity to reach millions and billions of people via smartphones and apps.

What I most love about the app business is not just this unlimited, fast growth potential but the freedom and fun you can have in the journey. You can choose to work from anywhere, anytime using teams across the world. I am passionate about creating more fun and freedom in my life and the lives of others. One needs to learn, grow, and evolve to have more fun and freedom. Growth by itself is not the goal. What is the point if you are learning and growing but never have any fun and the freedom to choose in life?

I believe the app business is one of the smartest ways to create a life of freedom and fun. My hope is that this book will give you the confidence and clarity to pursue your app-business dreams and impact the world positively with your idea.

WHO IS THIS BOOK FOR?

This book is written for aspiring entrepreneurs, business owners, corporate professionals, and the "average Joes" who desire to create more freedom, fun, and growth in their life by creating a successful app business. It is for those with one or more app ideas and wondering what their next step should be. It is for those stuck in nine-to-five jobs and looking for smart ways to get out and live more.

YOU WILL LEARN

Most people underestimate what it takes to build successful apps. They read the app success stories in the media and assume it is all about having the right idea at the right time. Building an app business has much more to it. This book gives you the knowledge you need to take full ownership for your app success.

You will learn about the various things involved in going from an idea to a profitable business including validating your idea, different options for building your app, raising funds, marketing, and maintaining your app with references to many real-world examples from companies like Uber, Airbnb, Facebook, etc. that you can relate to.

It will also help you set realistic expectations of what is involved in building a successful app business, so your journey does not have many unpleasant surprises.

Building an app business is very different to building a traditional business. This book is the first of its kind written specifically to help early-stage app entrepreneurs be successful.

HOW TO READ THIS BOOK

Each section of this book focuses on a specific topic. If you are new to both the entrepreneurship world and the app world, you will find the entire book very useful and insightful. But depending on your experience with apps and entrepreneurship, you may choose to skip or quickly skim some sections. For example, the first chapter is all about self-belief as an entrepreneur. This is critical for first-time entrepreneurs but if you have already established successful businesses and have a high self-belief in yourself and your idea, you may choose to skip this section. Similarly, there is another section focused on app building/technical information. If you are a coder yourself, you may choose to skip that section and focus on other sections like "funding" and "marketing." So I recommend you to go through the table of contents and focus on sections that are most relevant to you.

Within each chapter, I have also provided exercises, templates, and questions. You will get the most value from the book by spending time doing the exercises and answering the questions. I have also provided the links for you to download the worksheets and templates.

You can use this book as a guide to decide:

- if app entrepreneurship is for you
- which idea you should work on
- if you are ready to execute your idea
- your best next steps to take your idea to market
- your best strategies and tactics to take your app to the next level

I wish you all the best to create more freedom, fun, and growth in your life.

B Kris

Founder, director—Appomate.com.au

SECTION 1: CAN I DO THIS?

This first section is all about YOU! I bet you love hearing that, and it is important, because the realisation of your app ultimately rests with you. In this section, we start out with the core elements you will need as an app entrepreneur to ensure the greatest likelihood of success for you and your app.

1. Believe you can

Everything starts with belief. Life is what we believe it to be. Many people with great ideas go nowhere because they are trapped by fear or self-doubt. They don't think they have the knowledge or resources to make it happen. They think it takes a special person with superhero app-abilities to become a successful app entrepreneur. In some ways, they are right—it does take a special person—but that special person is you! The truth is, your background and circumstances matter less than your belief in yourself and your idea, and your willingness to learn and grow along the journey.

There are many examples of people from all walks of life who have succeeded on the app journey—entrepreneurs who had no money, no technical knowledge, and no connections who succeeded big time.

Andrew Carnegie, the richest man in the world during his time, was born to a poor man who worked in a handloom factory, grew up in poverty, and went on to become a great industrialist because of his hard work and passion for learning.

Samuel Walton, the founder of Walmart supermarket chain, grew up during the Depression delivering newspapers. He was managing a variety store at 26 when he had the idea that he could run his own store. He took out a loan to buy his first store. The rest is history. Forbes ranked him as the richest in the U.S from 1982-89.

Jan Koum, who sold his app business, WhatsApp, for $19 billion to Facebook, was born and raised in a very poor family in Ukraine and migrated to the US when he was 16. He used to sweep the floor of a grocery store as a job, learned coding, worked as an engineer, and then quit his job to work on his idea.

One of the characteristics each of these people shared is that they all believed in their idea and vision. This belief fuelled the type of unending perseverance required to turn any worthwhile idea into a reality.

Whether you think you can or you can't—you're right
—Henry Ford

Believe you can—it is a choice. Take action and make it happen. Successful app entrepreneurs are the ones who go for it and persevere despite the challenges they face. You will need this attitude to turn your seed of an idea into the full-fledged, flourishing tree it can become.

2. Know your purpose

Successful people begin with the end in mind
—Steven Covey

Building an app business takes a lot of hard work and commitment. When a hurdle comes up, *why* will you push through it and keep going? A great read about the power of *why* is Simon Sinek's book *Start With Why*. In this book, Simon shows how the world's most successful people—like Steve Jobs, the Wright brothers, Martin Luther King, and others—were able to inspire people around them and achieve remarkable things. They all had a natural ability to start with their *why*—their purpose—which enabled them to lead and inspire people.

Why do you want to create your app business? What positive impact will it create in this world?

Let's take a look at the "why" of some great entrepreneurs.

Make the world more open and connected to bring people together—Mark Zuckerberg

To help people be more productive so they can achieve their greatest potential—Bill Gates, Microsoft

To be original and have serious fun in (my) journey through life and learn from (my) mistakes—Richard Branson, Virgin Group

To organise the world's information and make it universally accessible and useful—Larry Page and Sergey Brin, Google

Every leader's "why" is as unique as their DNA. When you connect with your "why" that is true to your heart, you will be inspired from within.

Knowing your "why" makes you a leader. How do you find your "why"? It requires getting in touch with your heart. You cannot find your why only by thinking from your head. You need to feel with your heart. You need to understand who you are as a person. It takes time. It takes work. There are numerous ways to get to know yourself. Meditation, journalling, self-reflection, working with a coach all can help to know yourself. For me, it was years of meditation and self-reflection. Dr. John Demartini's teachings also helped me greatly. When I did his value determination exercise, I identified freedom, fun, and growth among my top values. I am also a vision partner at The Entourage, Australia's number-one entrepreneur training company. At The Entourage, we spend a lot of time focusing on vision, mission, and values. The Entourage has kindly offered its members-only template for readers of this book to work through their own vision, mission and values. To get access to the templates, go to http://bit.ly/2rMvG1M.

My purpose is to create more freedom, fun, and growth for myself and for others. My business and everything I do is driven by this very purpose.

Do you know your purpose? Start today. Inquire within. I highly recommend this exercise at https://drdemartini.com/value_determination/determine_your_values. It may take days, months, or years but eventually you can find it. When you find it, you can feel it in your heart. Know that your purpose can evolve as you know yourself more and evolve as a person. Start with the first version and keep working on it. I know everything I share in this book is only based on what is true for me now and that it can change. It is important to remember that your purpose does not have to be this larger-than-life, change-the-world statement. It can be quite simple, like "to be a great teacher." It's about being aware of who you are, knowing what excites you, and what comes naturally to you.

3. Aspire to live bigger

A strong self-belief and a clear purpose are critical components of a strong foundation to begin the app creation process. But do you have to wait until you know your purpose? Did every successful entrepreneur know their purpose before they started? Definitely not.

So what gets people started? In his famous *Think and Grow Rich* book, Napoleon Hill wrote a full chapter on desire. In that chapter, he explains how desire is the starting point of most achievements in history.

As human beings, we all desire certain things. We desire to "live bigger." Let's take a look at the different categories of living bigger so you can get in touch with the desire that's close to your heart.

The five primary categories of living bigger

Money

When starting out in the entrepreneurial journey, almost everyone thinks the end game for developing an app is to increase the dollars in their pocket. Money is often the main reason that drives people to develop their app ideas in the early days. The thought of increased wealth and all things that come with it—new homes, cars, toys, etc.—are enough to get people started and moving forward. **Money brings you options in life that you never had before. It provides the freedom to do and have what you want. In many cases, however, people focus on their desire for more money until they make more than they need, and soon realise what they are really looking for is a lot different than just money.**

Time

Given the speed with which life is currently lived, time is one of the most valuable things we can gain back in our lives. Many people desire their time with family, friends, and loved ones more than anything else. Working in a full-time job may not provide you with the amount of time you desire to spend with your loved ones or to do the things you love. You may want to create an app business so you have a greater choice on how much time you want to spend on activities and when.

Experience

For a special few, the living bigger dream is to increase the calibre and variety of experiences life has to offer. Creating an app business is sure to bring new opportunities to experience people, places, and events you would not have the opportunity to experience any other way. Many people are passionate about certain hobbies or activities and they want to live and share their passion through their business.

Legacy

For some people, becoming world famous and creating a legacy gives more satisfaction than money, time, or experience. The desire to create a legacy drives people to do amazing things. Think about boxers who risk their life fighting, or young Olympians who spend all their time training to win championships. I am not saying that all sportsmen are only driven by the desire to be famous and create a legacy but for many this seems to be the motivating factor.

Happiness

In the end, it all comes down to this. Everyone seeks happiness in life. We think more money, more time, being famous, etc. will make us happy. After having all of that, we realise that the feeling of fulfilment and gratification is what really makes us happy. **Creation by itself gives that feeling of fulfilment and gratification. It comes from taking a concept that doesn't exist and creating something meaningful. It comes from you being the solution to the problem you see every day.** Often startups are created because of the founder's frustration about a problem they see. There are not many things more fulfilling than acting on your idea and being the change you want to see.

Whether you desire more money, time, fame, experiences, or happiness, creating a successful app business can provide you with all of that.

What you desire the most can also help you choose what type of app business you want to build. If you desire money or legacy the most, you may want to create a big, scalable app business like Facebook.

If you desire more time, you may create a buyable app, sell it for millions of dollars to a bigger company, and retire early like *Instagram founders in their mid-twenties selling their app business for a billion dollars to Facebook in 2012.*

If you desire experiences and living your passion the most, you may create a lifestyle app business around what you are passionate about. The Zumba founders are great examples of how any passion can be turned into a scalable and successful business. They also launched an app for the Zumba teachers to get access to a wide range of music for their Zumba classes and a dance party app for the customers to dance Zumba with a tablet.

4. Steps to living bigger

Your dreams of living bigger will not come true automatically when you start building your app. You need to work smart on your app business and on yourself. The growth of your app business is only limited by your growth. Here are a few key steps you can take to grow yourself and live bigger.

Keep learning

Your chances for substantial success increase as you continue to cultivate your mind through learning more. The mind is a unique and fascinating tool. Unlike the body, which typically hits its peak one day, the mind has a nearly infinite ability to learn, grow, and develop.

When I refer to learning here, I don't mean the academic learning you experienced through primary and secondary school. I mean the ability to think differently, or more broadly, in ways that ultimately have a significant impact on the app you develop, as well as your dream to live bigger.

Einstein was misquoted many times (and I'll attempt to do it again here) when he said, "We cannot solve our problems with the same level of thinking that created them." This is infinitely wise and could not be more applicable to app development. The whole idea behind new app concepts is to solve problems using thinking that is categorically different to how problems have been solved historically.

We cannot solve our problems with the same level of thinking that created them
—Albert Einstein

Looking briefly at Airbnb, we find the challenge of making extra money in a difficult economy by using assets you already have. While this problem can be met many ways, *Airbnb looked at it differently. They took a leap that people would be willing to rent out their homes, apartments, and rooms to complete strangers. The corresponding leap was that people would be willing to pay to stay in a stranger's home or room rather than commercially available options.* The worlds of modern technology and age-old accommodation problems were mashed up to create one of the world's most wildly successful apps. In the end, we have happy home owners and happy renters—the ideal win-win.

Become a learning machine. Every time you use an app, analyse it critically. What is good, what is bad? When you read app success stories, inquire why.

Google Alerts is a great tool to educate yourself with the latest in the business and technology world. Add keywords like *app startups, app entrepreneurship*, and many other relevant topics you will learn in this book to your Google Alert, and it will email you any information and news published in those topics.

I researched the main skills early stage entrepreneurs should master. I researched by looking online, by asking successful app entrepreneurs, and from my own observations of people I have worked with. This is what I found as some of the main skills you should master as an early stage app entrepreneur.

- Sales. In the early stages, all you have is a concept, an idea, or maybe a product, but with no users. You need to sell this idea to your friends, family, and team members to get them on board to support you. You need to sell the idea to your customers, to get buy-in. The most challenging sale of all is selling to the great people you want as partners and investors in your business. Sharpen your sales skills by taking courses and by working with mentors and coaches.

- Networking. In the app startup world, often what separates wildly successful entrepreneurs from the rest is who they know. You need to surround yourself with great people who have been there, done that. You can reach anyone in the world through people you meet. You need to master your networking skills to develop good relationships, build a great team, and have the right people to support you. You will be surprised by how much people are willing to help you. You will find that the most experienced and knowledgeable people are often the most approachable and willing to help.
- App business knowledge. The app startup world is very different from the traditional business world. You need to understand the way app products are built, sold, and monetised. The chapters of this book will help you learn this very topic.

Learning does not stop with knowledge and skills. The most powerful learning of all is learning about yourself. Reflect, journal, meditate, and ask for feedback from friends and colleagues to learn about yourself. Know your strengths, your weaknesses, what you love, what you hate, your values, and your purpose.

Below are five self-awareness questions you can ask your friends, family and colleagues that will greatly assist you to learn about yourself.

1. What do you think is my biggest strength?
2. What do you think is my biggest weakness?
3. What is one thing you can always rely on me for?
4. What is one thing you can never rely on me for?

5. What would be one piece of advice you would give me right now?

When my partner and I asked these self-awareness questions to each other while trekking to the beautiful Sealer's Cove in Victoria, Australia it took our relationship to the next level. I highly recommend this exercise and the trek down to stunning Sealer's Cove ☺. (Thanks to the leadership training company www.integrityandvalues.com where I first learned this exercise.)

Maintain a happy mind

The secret to happiness rests in your mind. I know—big concepts for an app book, right? But this is at the heart of the living bigger movement. We all want to be happier and have fun.

What if there were things you could do to bring the happiness you expect to result from your successful app to you RIGHT NOW? Well, you can.

While this book isn't here to provide you a happiness formula in detail, here is a prescription to move you in the direction of increased happiness. These five activities will help you feel the great feelings you expect your app to bring you—*before* you even do the work!

- Keep a gratitude journal. Every day, write three things you are grateful for. This brings into your consciousness all the good things in life you already have, and helps create a "glass half full" mentality that will serve you during future challenges, app-related or otherwise.
- Help other people. This has been shown to increase happiness levels—and who knows, the people you help might end up helping you achieve your dream (although that's not the only reason to give help).

Science has proven that when we help someone else, we feel better about ourselves. Feeling deflated because your app failed its first attempt in the App Store? Go do something nice for your partner, and it will lessen the stress.

- Exercise. Exercise has been proven to help stimulate the brain and bring about greater levels of satisfaction. Now, you already know this, so the real key is to find the type of exercise you enjoy! Yoga, dancing, cycling, swimming, UFC, basketball, walking—the list goes on and on. Find the thing you enjoy, and do it because you enjoy it, not because you think you have to. You'll see and feel the benefits quickly.

Those who do not find time to exercise now will have to find time for illness later
—Edward Smith Stanley

- Spend time with your top five. Relationships are critical to satisfaction in life. Identify the top five people who inspire you, lift you up, and/or you aspire to be like, and spend more time with them. You'll be glad you did.
- Set goals. This is a big enough category to merit more attention. You will read more about goal setting in the next section.

By the way, **scientists have proven that humans are more creative, collaborate more effectively, and are more productive in a happy state of mind. So instead of waiting for what you want to become happy, be happy to get what you want.**

Set goals and make plans

To achieve your dream, you will benefit greatly from describing what it looks like in as much detail as possible and writing it down. **Did you know that written goals are ten times more likely to be achieved than goals that are just in your head and don't make it to pen and paper?** There are many studies on the power of setting and writing down goals, but here is one to help pound home the point.

In his book, *What They Don't Teach You in Harvard Business School*, Mark McCormack wrote about a 1979 study conducted on Harvard MBA students. The students were asked, "Have you set clear, written goals for your future and made plans to accomplish them?" Only 3% of the students had written goals. Ten years later, the study revisited the students to see how they were going. The ten-year check-up revealed that **the 3% who had documented goals were earning, on average, 10 times as much as the other 97% combined!** It might be time to put pen to paper around your app goals and, just for good measure, throw in a few other goals around health, relationships, and finance. You won't regret it.

Take actions

Were you ever in a location where you needed a map to find how to get to your destination? The map by itself is not going to get you where you want to go. You need to put one foot in front of the other, or get in the car and hit the accelerator, or call an Uber; all of these approaches require action on your part. Once you've set your app goals and a high-level plan (your map), you need to take the required action to get to your destination. Break down your plan into detailed action steps and keep implementing your actions every day. Learning, planning, and goal setting without implementing your actions is not going to get you any further. You learn the most from taking actions. The number-one reason that stops people from taking action is fear of failure. Failure teaches you faster than anything else would.

I have not failed. I've just found 10,000 ways that won't work
—Thomas Edison.

So observe yourself. Are you taking regular action, or just dreaming, learning, and talking without any real action due to fear of failure? **Take at least one step every single day that will move you towards your goal.**

Set your brain for success

Successful people are obsessed with their success. They don't complain about working long hours. They act on their plan and work towards their goal. Are there ways you can wire your brain to stay focused and automatically take actions in the direction of your goals?

There are numerous scientific studies about how to program your brain by using different media to feed information to your brain's RAS (Reticular Activating System). RAS is the part of the brain that filters which information we are tuned to, and as a result, controls our thoughts and actions. Here are some ways to tune your RAS so it filters information that supports your goals to your brain.

- Feed your "why" and your goals into your subconscious mind by creating a vison board. Find images that represent your goals, print them, frame them, and put them in a place you can see every day.
- Practice visualisation. Close your eyes to see and feel

all your goals and dreams coming true. In one of the conferences I attended, I heard from this lady who said she grew her finger back that she lost in an accident by visualising it growing back every single day for many months. While that is an extraordinary case, it goes to highlight the power of visualisation.

Build a great team

People see successful apps and say, "Wow, what a great idea. Wish I came up with that idea." But it is never just the idea—it's always the people behind it who turn the idea into a successful business through great execution. A business will never outgrow its founders and the team behind it.

In his book, *Good to Great*, author Jim Collins explains the findings of five years of research by his team on what it takes to change a good company into a great company, i.e. generate stock returns that exceeded the general stock market by at least three times over a 15-year period. His research found that the leaders of great companies start with "who." They work on building the right team before doing anything else. If your team cannot execute your idea better than anyone else can, then you have no reason to win big. Instead of spending energy on protecting your idea, focus on building a great team by inspiring people with your idea and your purpose. By team, I mean your founding partners, investors, employees, and suppliers. When you know that even if someone copies your idea, they will not be able to execute it like your team can, you are on the road to success.

The rest of this book will educate you about apps and help you understand the type of action you need to take to grow your app idea into a successful app business and help find your way to your dream. Before you start reading the rest of the book, take some time out to reflect and answer these key questions based on what you've learned so far.

5. Exercise:

1. Belief: On a scale of 1-10, how strongly do I believe in myself and my idea?

2. Purpose: Why do I want to build this app? How will my app business impact the world positively?

3. Desire:
   a. On a scale of 1-10, how strong is my desire to live bigger?

b. What do I desire the most? Based on that, what type of app business do I want to create?

4. Learn and implement: On a scale of 1-10, how willing am I to learn and take action every day?

5. Goals: What are some of my short-term (one to two years) and long-term (five to ten years) goals?

6. Team: Who are the top five to ten people I would like on my team?

SECTION 2:
IS MY IDEA GOOD?

6. Creating winning app ideas

There are quite a few people including me who will tell you, "In the app entrepreneurship world, the ideas don't matter. Execution is the game." While it is definitely true that execution is paramount, executing a bad idea won't get you very far either.

Your winning app idea must align with your *why*, as this will feed you when times are lean. Your idea would ideally:

- Solve a significant problem common to a large number of people; and
- Serve a universal need.

You have a greater opportunity for massive success if the need is not restricted to a particular location, language, or culture.

Based on passion and frustration:

We discussed that many startups are created based on the founder's passion or frustration. Answer these questions.

- What are you passionate about?
- What kind of app would you pay for in your area of passion?

- What big problems have frustrated you on a regular basis that you really want to solve?
- What complaints do you hear about all the time from your friends and family?

For example, MyFitnessPal founder Mike Lee was on a diet to lose weight for his wedding. Frustrated by the use of pen and paper to track his diet, he decided to build his own solution to his frustration. He launched the website version in Sep 2005, then launched the apps. On February 4, 2015, MyFitnessPal was purchased and acquired by athletic apparel maker, Under Armour, for $475 million. MyFitnessPal had 80 million users at the time.

Based on expertise:

Your idea may also be based on your professional expertise and experience. Lots of apps are born out of a founder's experience in an industry, which leads to a discovery of a much more effective and efficient way of doing something through the right app.

- What is your subject matter expertise?
- How can you share your expertise with the world at scale?

Based on trends:

Your idea may be based on following trends or borrowing ideas. Look at the top apps charts. What kind of apps are making the most revenue? What are the trends and successful apps in other industries? Which successful trends interest you the most? What problems are these successful apps solving?

One thing common to all these methods to create winning ideas is that it should solve a significant problem and add huge value. People often make the mistake of starting from a solution or even worse starting from a feature. Start with a problem, a significant one that needs solving to increase your chances of success. Research the solutions available in the market and then refine your ideas.

There are also some websites where you can find good app ideas. http://www.ideaswatch.com/ is one such website.

Once you shortlist some ideas you want to work on, you can then validate them to choose which one you want to work on. The next section shows you how to validate your ideas.

7. Validate your idea's greatness

How good is your idea? It is wise to assess the demand for your idea before you invest a lot of time and money into your app.

Does your idea have the elements to become a successful app?

What do the world's most successful apps have in common? My research team and I spent some time digging into this question, and here is what we found. Your awesome app idea has a much greater probability of success if it incorporates these four elements.

1. Meet a universal need

A universal need is something that transcends culture, language, location, and time. There are things which make us all human beings, like:

- The need for food and shelter
- The need for safety and security
- The need for connection and belonging

- The need for recognition and appreciation
- The need for skill mastery, achievement, and freedom.

For example, social networking and instant messenger apps are among the most successful because they fulfil the need for connection and belonging. Gaming apps help people feel they are mastering some skills and give a sense of achievement. Sharing apps, like Airbnb and Uber, help people save money and make money, and in doing so, help meet their needs for financial security and freedom.

2. Tap into the habit loop

All successful apps tap into the human operating system by making some element of their app part of a regular routine for its users. In many cases, this leverages the first element of meeting a universal need. Successful apps utilise the habit loop of cue-routine-reward. They know and define the triggers or cues for users to use their app, and include clear rewards for the habit. For example, Facebook notifications to your smartphone when someone likes or comments on your posts and photos is the cue. The feeling of being bored also acts like an internal cue. User starts scrolling their infinite newsfeed—the routine. The engagement and the feeling of being liked or recognised is the reward. If you haven't read the book *Power of Habits* yet, I highly recommend it. What you can learn from that book is just mind-blowing. The author shows how many companies have made their product a habit for their consumers. Another great book about creating habit-forming products is *Hooked* by Nir Eyal.

3. Incorporate network effects and viral loops

In the network effect, a product becomes more valuable and useful when more people use it (this also plays an important role in your chosen revenue model; see next point). Facebook is great when all your friends are in there with you. WhatsApp is cool when all your friends, local and international, are using it, as it makes communication quicker, easier, and more fun. This motivates users to invite their contacts to use the app.

A viral loop is created when there is a clear need or incentive for one user to invite others. The best apps build incentives for their users to invite more users.

Dropbox offers free storage when a user invites a friend to use Dropbox. Uber gives you taxi credit when you share your experience with your friends and invite them to use it. Airbnb offers hosts money for introducing new hosts to Airbnb.

4. Pick the right revenue model

Your idea increases in greatness when you have a clear approach to making money through the app. Revenue split, subscription, in-app advertising, and in-app purchases are the four most successful revenue models. We will discuss the different revenue models in detail in chapter 9.

- *Revenue Split:* Apps that make the most money are the ones which create a marketplace and help others make a lot of money—for a small cut. These app companies help their customers make money, and in doing so, split the revenue. *Uber takes a 25% commission of what passengers pay the drivers, Airbnb takes a 6-to-12% commission from the hosts, and Spotify, up to 30% commission from the music producers/publishers.*

- *In-App Advertising*: This is when you build a huge user base (audience) and then charge advertisers for clicks and views by your users. Facebook makes billions of dollars every year in advertisement revenue from businesses publishing their ads in the Facebook platform.

- *Subscription:* Charge an ongoing fee for the service your app offers. This is a very common model for software as a service-type app; for example, *Xero is an accounting software/app for businesses averaging at about $50 a month. With over a million subscribers, Xero's revenue was US$141.2 million in FY16. However, they are heavily reinvesting all the money and made a net loss in FY16. It could also work for any type of app; for example, Lumosity, a cognitive games app that focuses on improving different functions of your brain, provides access to the app's 50+ brain games for a monthly subscription fee starting from $11.99. The app claims to have 85 million users across the world with an annual revenue crossing US $24 million in 2016.*

- *In-App Purchases:* In this model, you make your app free to use but have special features within your app for users to buy as in-app purchases. Candy Crush Saga is a multibillion-dollar app which uses in-app purchases with only 3% of the customers who pay and the remaining 97% users use the app for free and do not pay a cent. This app demonstrates the power of human need (for sense of achievement), habit loop, and network effects. We will discuss more about this app in chapter 9 on revenue models.

How many of these four success elements does your app idea tick?

1. **Does your idea satisfy a universal need?**
2. **Can it be habit forming?**
3. **Is there a network effect advantage or incentives to create a viral loop?**
4. **Does it employ one of the four top revenue models?**

8. Get the timing right

Do you know the single biggest reason why tech startups succeed or fail? I don't believe there is just one reason, may be one of the important reasons. Bill Gross, founder of Idealab, did a TED talk about just this topic.

He wanted to find out what would be the single, most important reason why startups succeed, and explored five factors: the idea, the team, the business model, the funding, and the timing.

He defined "timing" this way:

- Is the idea too early and the world isn't ready for it?
- Is the timing just right?
- Is the idea too late, and the field is already flooded with competitors?

Bill Gross studied hundreds of businesses, successful and otherwise, and concluded that the number-one contributor to both success and failure is *timing*. Are consumers really ready for what you have to offer them?

For example, *Airbnb began during the height of the recession, when people really needed extra money, and the idea of renting out their own home to a stranger became more acceptable. YouTube didn't even have a business model when it first started, but it was launched just as 50% of America could access broadband and stream videos fast: brilliant timing.*

You'll know that the timing is right when your target market responds well to your app idea. But building and launching your app just to see the response can be very risky and expensive. So I have suggested some tactics that will allow you, to some extent, to find out if the timing is right without having to build your product.

Use Google Keyword Planner and Google Trends analysis. These tools tell you the demand for different keywords in Google searches, and thus gives you a good idea of the demand for your idea. What keywords would represent the demand for your product? Simply type in the keywords that represent your idea into the below URLs.

A. https://adwords.google.com.au/KeywordPlanner
   https://www.google.com.au/trends/

B. Google surveys allows you to get opinions from consumers across the world by simply asking questions. List the assumptions you are making about your target customers, their needs and wants. Define the age and demographics of your target user, and use the Google survey tool to let Google find the answers to your questions about your target market and the real demand for your idea from the millions of users in their database. https://www.google.com/analytics/surveys

C. Create a landing page with some mock-ups of your app screens, and sell your app before creating your app. You can even simply sell your solution on a landing page without app screens. There are many landing page template websites (Instapages, Unbounce) to quickly set up landing pages. Drive people to the page using ad campaigns. Have users subscribe to receive updates about the app launch, or to receive an invite to use the app when it is launched.

These methods can help you understand the demand for your idea before you make a significant investment in money or time. Another simple but very effective method is to simply call or meet your target users and talk to them in person. **This is what Uber's CEO Travis did when he first came up with the idea. He cold-called taxi drivers to get their feedback,** and when three out of every 10 calls showed interest, he knew there was a demand for his idea.

9. Establish how you will make money

Understand app revenue models. Your idea is not complete without a suitable revenue model. We explored the most successful ones in a previous section. This chapter shows you the possible revenue models in an app business.

Paid apps

This is the basic model, in which you sell your app for a listed price on the App Store or Google Play Store. You choose a price from available price tiers, which are anywhere from 99 cents to $999 USD. Most paid apps are under $10; there are few expensive apps. *The Agro Ezi app is one of them, priced at $1599 AUD.*

This model works well for game and utility apps. *Minecraft Pocket at $9 per app made $326 million dollars in 2013 from paid downloads. Shiftworker, a calendar app for shift workers at $2.99, which topped the App Store charts for few months in 2015, is a good example of a paid utility app.*

The advantage of this model is that it provides quick cash flow. You get the money as soon as someone downloads the app—but at the same time, it is not easy to convince people to pay, as there are many free apps. Your app must be unique and top quality for users to pay for it. Currently (2016), fewer than 10% of all apps in the App Store are paid apps. **For paid apps, the App Store and Google Play Store take 30% of the revenue as a transaction fee, and pay you the remaining 70%.**

Free app with in-app advertising

In this model, you let people use the app for free and build a large audience. You sell advertisement space in your app, using ad networks like Admob, Flurry, etc. These ad networks connect publishers (you, the app builder) with advertisers and manage the whole process of placing and managing advertisements. They take a cut of the money paid by the advertisers and pay the remaining to the app publishers (you).

If you are big enough, you can also build your own ad serving platform within the app. This gives you the flexibility to decide the price and other terms of advertisement with the advertisers.

Facebook follows this revenue model, and has its own advertisement management platform. Facebook's quarterly ad revenue exceeded $4 billion in 2015.

This model works well for social networking and gaming apps where people essentially want to kill time. It does not work very well for utility apps, as it might annoy users when they are trying to get things done.

Freemium/in-app purchases

In this model, you list the app for free, and users can upgrade to a paid version or buy items (more features or physical goods) via in-app purchases. The premise is you engage the users, make them love your app, and have them pay to get more.

This model works really well for gaming apps where users need to pay to access advanced levels or special powers. *For example, Candy Crush Saga made $1.3 billion via in-app purchases in 2014 from 3% of its users. Dating apps are another example where you can browse your matches for free, but need to pay to contact them.*

For example, the famous Tinder dating is a free app. Users can find matches for free for an unlimited period of time but can also upgrade to Tinder Plus which gives them access to a "rewind" feature which will allow users to go back to a profile they swiped before and a "Passport" feature which allows them to use the app in multiple locations when they are travelling. Users can also swipe right (say yes) to an unlimited number of profiles in the Plus whereas it's limited to a certain number every 12 hours in the free plan. It also has a "boost" feature for an in-app purchase that users can buy to get their profile in the top.

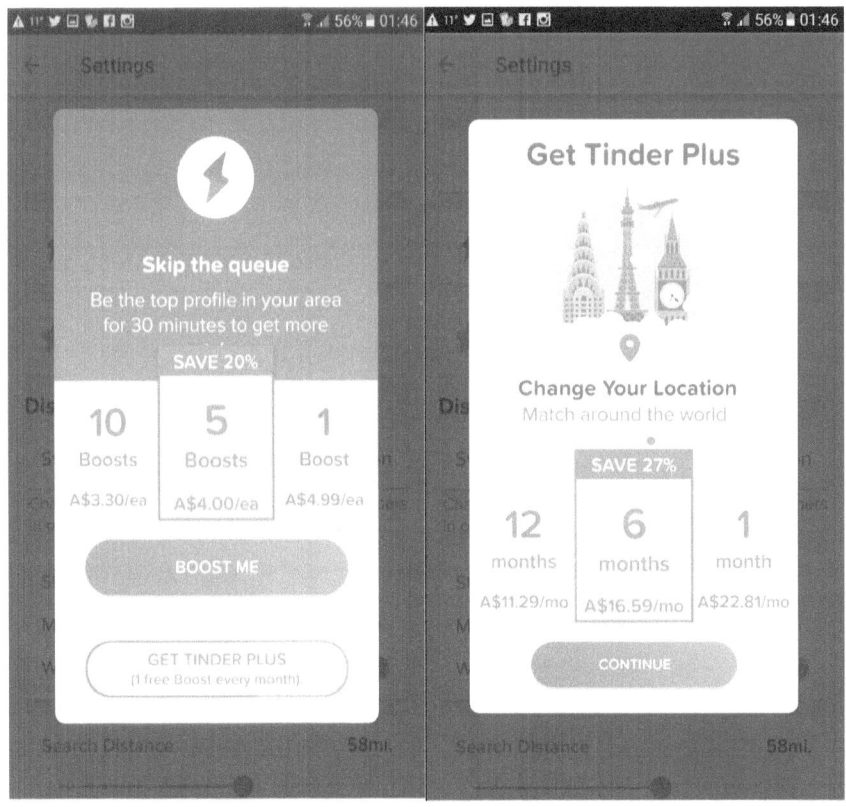

In the 2016 Q1 report, the parent company Match Group reported that Tinder had over 50 million users world-wide and one million of them were in the paid Tinder Plus plan.

One advantage is that the Freemium model offers a low barrier to entry for downloads (user acquisition)—but finding the sweet spot for paid features takes experimenting. Too few features for free might create a high churn rate, whereas too many features for free may not encourage the user to buy. The App Store and Play Store takes 30% of your in-app purchase revenue as well. From Tinder's example, you can see only 2% of the users upgraded from free app to paid app. So you have to cover the cost of 98% of your (free) users with the revenue from your 2% paid users.

In-app purchases may also involve physical goods, like clothes, accessories, etc. Since an App Store account is used for payment, it makes the buying process easy and quick for the buyer. The good news is (at least at time of this writing) there is no 30% transaction fee charged by the App Store for physical goods.

Subscription

In this model, the user pays a monthly or annual subscription fee to use the app. Most of the time, these apps offer a one-week or one-month free trial to allow users to "try before they buy."

The subscription model is best suited for business and enterprise apps like CRM, invoicing apps, and media/entertainment apps like music and news apps.

The advantage is a high lifetime value of customers due to ongoing revenue. On the other hand, users expect great customer support, 100% uptime, continuous updates, and a bug-free app when they pay an ongoing subscription fee.

Dropbox, Xero, and a lot of business software as a service apps use this model. Consumer apps in entertainment and games can also use this model. *For example, Spotify uses this model. In the free version, you can only listen to songs online and* *there are advertisements that you cannot skip. In the premium version, you can download and listen to the songs offline and the listening is uninterrupted with no advertisements. The company was founded in 2006 in Sweden and launched their app in October 2008; Spotify topped a revenue of $2 billion in 2015.*

One of my favorite apps, Audible, uses this model too. You can either buy individual audio books via in-app purchases or you can pay a monthly subscription fee starting at $15 to get free credits. You can use the credits to buy any book. With credits, you can buy the audio books at a discounted flat price but you have to use your credits every month. It works great for users who want to listen to audio books regularly. I highly recommend this app. When I am driving, cooking, travelling, my Audible app is great company.

Revenue split

In this model, you create a marketplace, enable others to make money, and then take a commission of the money they make. These apps are free to download and use.

Uber and Airbnb are the two popular apps using this model. *Uber takes a 20-to-25% commission of the money the drivers make. Airbnb charges 6%-to-12% of the money made by people renting their property.* This is a fast-growing revenue model because your users do the sales for you to make themselves more money. The more money they make, the more you make.

On the flip side, you need to ensure that the buyers are getting the service/product they are promised in the app. You can make them sign disclaimers and protect yourself legally, but if the sellers of product and service do not do the right thing, it will affect your brand. *For example, though Uber does not own the fleet or employ the drivers, they follow a very strict process before allowing drivers to use the Uber app to ensure they are reliable and provide great service to their customers. They check the driver's driving history, police clearance, the condition of their car, etc. to ensure the quality of the service.*

Build and flip

In this model, you build an app and sell it for a decent profit in marketplaces to someone who can build further on it. *FEInternational, flippa.com, and Chupamobile.com are marketplaces where you can sell your app source code and app business to other developers.*

This model allows a faster return than other models, but the opportunity is very limited. Low risk provides low reward. People buy code to save time and money in development.

Build a brand and sell to a strategic buyer

In this model, you build a successful app with a huge user base and sell the app to a bigger company who can leverage your app and your users. These bigger companies are called strategic buyers because their existing business model, customers, or some resource they have allow them to derive many times more value from your app than you can. For example, you have built a road trip planning and route optimisation app with 100,000 users who love the app. Google Maps can buy this app and sell the app to their millions of Google Maps users. They can make more money much faster than you can so they will be more than happy to pay a hefty premium for your app.

- Microsoft bought Minecraft for $2.5 billion in cash.
- Yahoo bought Tumblr for $1.1 billion because Yahoo was behind in the social media game and also did not have many millennials in their customer base. Tumblr provided the opportunity for them to achieve both.
- Facebook bought WhatsApp for $19 billion based

on their extraordinary user engagement metrics and access to their huge user base in markets like Asia where Facebook did not have a huge market share.

Knowing these seven revenue models, which do you think works best for you and your app? Keep in mind that your model can be a combination of one or more revenue models. For instance, Spotify has a free version that uses in-app advertising, and also offers a subscription model for an ad-free premium version. They use the revenue from ads and subscription fees to pay royalties to music artists and distributors while taking a 30% commission. So they have combined three of the seven models explained above.

10. Define your MVP

Many startups waste precious time and money by working in the wrong order: they want to perfect the product before they establish the viability of the product concept.

Many app entrepreneurs start with what they think customers want, argue over what they think customers value, and, after months or years of hard work, spend tens of thousands of dollars and build a product only to find that customers couldn't care less about it.

So how do you avoid falling into this trap? Do things in the right order: use MVP.

Startups can minimise risk by creating a Minimal Viable Product (MVP). A Minimum Viable Product does not eliminate the risk altogether but maximises your return on the risk you are taking. **It is the approach of first building and launching an app with a minimum set of features, with the primary purpose of gaining user feedback.**

The term MVP seems to have been coined by Frank Robinson of Sync Dev in 2001. He defined MVP as that unique product that maximises return on risk for the customer. It was Eric Ries who popularised the term in his book *The Lean Startup*.

To appreciate Eric Ries' definition of MVP, you first need to understand the "lean startup" principle and the concept of *validated learning*.

According to lean startup principle, the main thing that differentiates startups from big companies is that in a startup, the viability of the product and business model needs to be proven for every product. The initial focus is on learning and proving viability, not on profits or revenues, like big companies.

Learning is validated by measuring data, and accelerated by applying that data as the product is built. Ries called it the "Build-Measure-Learn loop." According to him, "the minimum viable product is that version of a new product which allows a team to collect the maximum amount of validated learning with the least effort."

As an example, Ries notes that Zappos founder Nick Swinmurn wanted to test the assumption that customers were ready and willing to buy shoes online. Instead of building a website, holding an inventory and marketing it, Swinmurn approached local shoe stores, took pictures of their inventory, posted the pictures online, bought the shoes from the stores, and shipped them directly to customers. Swinmurn deduced that customer demand was present, and Zappos would eventually grow into a billion-dollar business selling shoes online. (By the way, the company grew and chose to focus on a new purpose, which was delivering happiness. These guys understood what their live bigger dream was, and refocused to make it a reality. In his book, *Delivering Happiness*, Zappos CEO Tony Hsieh shares how focusing on "delivering happiness" as the higher purpose helped him achieve success in business and life.)

Some simple examples of MVPs include:

- AngelList. AngelList is a marketplace that connects startups and investors. The problem they're solving is that it's hard for both sides of the marketplace to find each other. To test and prove their assumptions, they created an MVP: they made manual email introductions to startups looking for funding and investors looking for investments.
- Uber. The MVP version of the famous taxi app, which is now the fastest-growing app in the world, was launched in 2010. The app simply allowed users to find drivers. It didn't have any fancy features you see today like fare splitting, rewards, etc. Also, there was no app for drivers. In the early days of Uber (Ubercabs), Uber's CEO Travis Kalanik himself was cold-calling cab drivers, met them, and signed them up.

Acquiring the MVP mindset

You need the right mindset to build the MVP version of your app. If you are a perfectionist, then prepare yourself now, because you won't be creating the perfect app. The goal is to release a product as soon as possible, and to learn what you need to learn. Accelerated learning should be your number-one objective, and MVP is your best method for achieving this end.

One of the common concerns associated with MVP is that releasing an imperfect app too soon will alienate customers, and you'll lose them forever. This concern assumes you already know who your customers are, how to reach them, and that they care about your product so much that they would be turned off forever. The good news is this isn't proving to be true; most product startups are taking the MVP path, and success has not been shown to be hampered by early versions.

The benefits of releasing the first stage of an app fast, without its bells and whistles, are quick feedback, knowing what your customers really value, and testing all your assumptions. It's important not to get caught up in details of branding, cosmetic bugs, and the like while launching your MVP. You must think big for the long term, but think basic for the short term.

MVP benefits

Having fewer features allows you to:

- Test your assumptions about the product and market with minimum investment
- Get the product to market faster
- Reduce wasted time and money in building the wrong features
- Reduce development, quality assurance, and customer support costs
- Make learning easier.

MVP assumptions

- You are building a product that is new to the market. You don't know if demand exists for the product
- You have a great team to build and sell your vision
- You can implement a Build-Measure-Learn loop by implementing analytics to gather data, and make changes to the app quickly based on that data.

MVP challenges

- The founder's passion for the idea and the team members' pride in their knowledge and experience stacks one idea on top of another, resulting in a big features list for the MVP. You need to be discerning and say "no" or "later" to some good ideas.

- It's difficult to choose one segment of your customer base to test. Your end product might fit a wide swath of customer types, but you need to focus on one segment for the MVP, and build to their preference. Similarly, amidst the growing number of platforms and devices (iOS, Android, Windows, web), you must limit the MVP to one or two platforms.

- The challenge is to build the smallest product but at the same time provide an enjoyable customer experience. **What is the minimum user experience your customers would expect from your app?** *How* **the app works is as important as or more important than** *what* **the app does. App users are used to great apps. MVPs, though still small, need to be built to an excellent standard. Users will not use apps unless they are easy and intuitive to use.**

Your focus is to provide the most important features and functionality to show the user what is possible, and get feedback that teaches you about your product viability.

MVP is not necessary for every startup. For example, your app idea could be based on an existing app and making it better. You already know there is demand for the product, and your strategy may simply be to create a superior product and offer it at the same or cheaper price. In such a case, MVP may not play a significant role, and you may have to create a full-blown product with all the bells and whistles. You have to know what you know as facts and what your assumptions are. MVP is more useful when there are more assumptions.

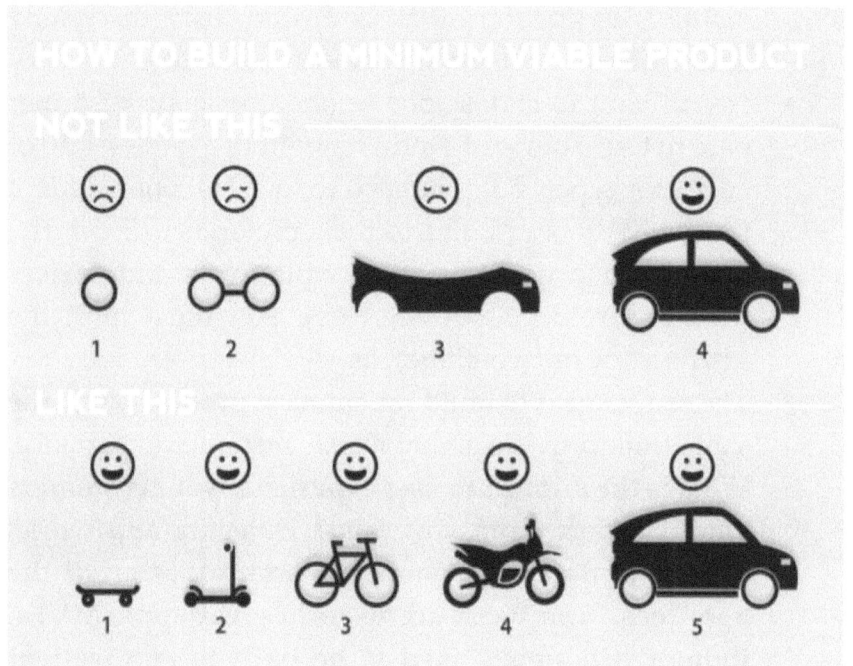

See the fast monkeys blog.

In Section 2, we discussed different methods to test the potential of your app idea: the four elements common to hugely successful apps, testing if the timing is right, picking the right revenue model and using MVP to test your assumptions. I also highly recommend these two books, *The Lean Startup* by Eric Ries and *Hooked* by Nir Eyal, which will help you further in refining your idea, app features, and deciding what your MVP should be.

SECTION 3:
I AM NOT A TECHIE

One of the common concerns or fears for people wanting to get into app entrepreneurship is that they have no idea about coding or how it works and therefore they think it is not for them. You don't have to know coding to be a successful app entrepreneur. There are many successful app entrepreneurs who aren't coders. Let's take a look at some of them.

- *At age 25, Evan Spiegel, the co-founder of Snapchat, was reported by Forbes as the world's youngest billionaire. He did not seem to have any advanced programming skills.*
- *Jack Ma founded China's largest B2B e-commerce website, Alibaba, and is a billionaire now, but when he borrowed $2000 to set it up, he knew nothing about computers or even emails.*
- *Melody McCloskey, the founder of StyleSeat, a successful marketplace app, knew no coding when she built the first version of the app by outsourcing it to freelance developers.*
- *Alex Turnbull, the founder of Groove, a helpdesk software, was not a coder and did not have a technical co-founder, yet he took his company to multimillion-dollar revenue by outsourcing the app development to an agency.*
- *The man himself, Steve Jobs, was never a programmer and did not do any coding since the early days when they coded the Apple 1 OS. In fact, Steve Wozniak, the cofounder of Apple, once said Steve Jobs knew no technology, let alone programming.*

Though these guys did not know programming, they had some understanding of technology or product development. It is important you have some level of technical knowledge and understanding of the development process in order to choose the right team, make the right decisions, manage the tech team, and produce the desired outcome.

In this chapter, you will learn the jargon and technical essentials to make informed decisions when choosing your development partner and technologies.

11. The app-development process

Building an app is similar to building a house in a lot of ways (but it is also very different to building a house in a lot of ways). You have to create the plan and lay the foundation, step by step, stage by stage. Let's take a look at various stages involved in building an app.

Requirement gathering and analysis

This is the initial phase, when you and the whole team are involved in the development brainstorm and analyse the requirements of the app. The goal of this phase is to ensure everyone not only understands the requirements, but to produce a document that captures all the requirements in detail. Companies may use various terms, like SRS (system requirement specification), BRD (business requirement document), or PRD (product requirement document). Most app development companies have a "business analyst" or a "product manager" who owns the process of gathering, analysing, and documenting requirements. In your documentation, make sure the following details are captured.

- High-level goals of your app. Why you are building the app—what is the objective? This is developed based on your answers in Section 1.
- Functional requirements. These describe the details of the features and functions available in your app. This is the most important and detailed part of your documentation. The term "User stories" or "Use cases" are popular in the app industry as a way to document requirements. *User stories* are short, simple descriptions of a feature told from the perspective of the person who desires the feature, usually a user or customer of the system. They typically follow a simple template: *As a <type of user>, I want <some goal> so that <some reason>.* For instance, "As a videographer, I want to be able to upload my video into the app, so I can back it up and never lose it."
- Technical and non-functional requirements, which are not functions, but describe how the app should work. For example, "The app needs to work without internet." "All pages need to load in less than five seconds."
- You can download our BRD template at Appomate. com.au/resources

UI/UX design

In this phase, the wireframes of your app are designed by UX designers. Wireframes are skeleton drawings showing the different buttons, functions, and info in the different pages of the app. This is an important part in developing your app. With millions of apps in the App Store, what's crucial is no longer what the app can do—it's how the app does it.

Is it easy, engaging, and intuitive to use? A professional UX designer takes your documentation and turns it into screens and mockups of the app. UXPin, Balsamiq, and InVision are some UX wireframing tools available in the market.

Typically, a branding expert designs the logo, colour, and fonts for your app brand based on your target user and their goals. *User persona* is great tool to workshop and understand your target user. These branding elements are put in a single document called a *style guide*. Your brand's style guide is then applied to your wireframes to get the desired User Interface of your app. At this stage, you can pretty much see and feel the end product you are building, even though no coding has been done yet.

Development

This is the stage where the programmers look at the documentation (BRD) and the UI designs to code the app features and functions and bring the idea to life. It involves the development of different components of an app, like the front-end, back-end, API (Application Programming Interface), etc. It often involves multiple developers, as the app may involve multiple technologies.

Testing

Many businesses have testers, or a QA (quality assurance) team, who test the app end to end to ensure it works as per the expectations in the documentation and design. With the rising variety of devices and operating systems, you need to ensure your team is testing your app for a range of devices and operating systems. The more your app is tested, the more reliable it is. It is a good idea to invite your friends and family to test the app as well and give you feedback.

Launch

This is the final step after the developers have fixed all the testing feedback. It is not uncommon for apps to go live with some small bugs. This stage involves uploading the apps to the App Store and Google Play Store to make it available for download and use.

Now that you understand the main steps involved in the development of an app, let's look at the two key development methodologies or approaches in app development.

12. App development methodologies

Waterfall approach

In this approach, the steps of analyse, design, develop, test, and go live are done in sequence, one after the other. You complete each step for the entire scope of your app before proceeding to the next step. This approach is ideal when the app is relatively small and the requirements are clear and not expected to change quickly. It keeps the process in control in terms of time and budget, but does not offer much flexibility to changes in market conditions. If the entire development is expected to take less than six months, and the requirements are not subject to change, the waterfall approach may be suitable.

But if the app is big and is expected to take longer than six months, a lot of things can change during that development time, like technology, design trends, competition, market demand, etc. The requirements you capture in the document at the beginning may be less relevant by the time you test the app at the end of the project.

The waterfall approach might suit bigger projects in some cases, for example, when you are migrating or upgrading an existing system within an organisation. The requirement might be just to replicate the features of the existing system, and the changes in the market may not have an impact, as the app is not in the open market. Using the waterfall development approach allows developers to provide a fixed quote and timeline based on a fixed set of requirements.

Agile approach

In this approach, an iterative approach is followed for building the app. Instead of going step by step for the entire app, you do it for small parts of the app, building the app in an iterative approach. Each iteration goes through the analysis, design, develop, and test phases to produce a small piece of working software at the end of each iteration. The software grows as you move forward from one iteration to the next. This approach encourages flexibility and allows quick response to change. It is very suitable for projects where there are a lot of assumptions on what is required, and when the market conditions change regularly. The challenge with the agile approach is that you cannot have a fixed deadline and a fixed budget because the requirements are subject to change.

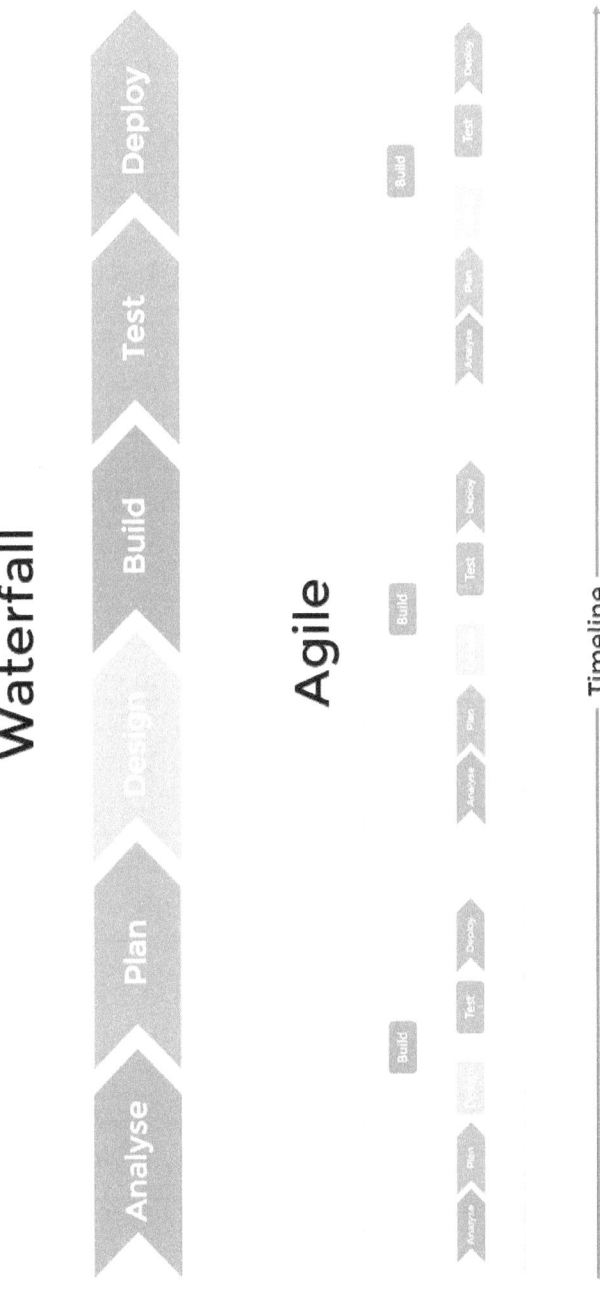

With your understanding of these two approaches, you (with your developer) can make an informed decision on the right approach for your app. An agile approach is what experts (including me) recommend, because the world changes so fast. If you are bringing a completely new idea to the market, the agile approach is definitely better than the waterfall, because you don't really know what the users want. But if you are creating a product to replace what already exists, and there is nothing to validate and test, the waterfall can be a more efficient approach.

Waterfall	Agile
Fixed requirements during the project	Requirements can vary during the project
Favours fixed cost, fixed time. Upfront expectations can be set	Challenging to have fixed cost, fixed time as requirements are expected to change and evolve
Challenging to adopt to changes during development	Easy to adopt to changes during development. Changes are embraced
Suits when the requirements are already validated by users. Example: you are simply building a clone or migrating existing app to a new technology	Suits when you are building something new in the market and user validation is required
Wait till end for a working software	Working software versions released during development
Suits when you need to keep the budget low for an initial launch	Suits a lean startup approach where you constantly update the product based on feedback

13. Types of apps

The other important technical aspect you need to understand to build a successful app business are the different types of apps. Often app entrepreneurs are bombarded with options of mobile responsive websites, mobi sites, native apps (iOS, Android), cross-platform apps, and hybrid apps. Different developers recommend different options, based on their experience and expertise. It is critical you understand what each means, and the pros and cons of each type, so you can make the right decision for your app.

Two types of web-based apps

Mobile responsive websites

A responsive website automatically responds and fits itself to the user's screen size. The design makes use of fluid, proportion-based grids and flexible images, so all the elements in a page automatically resize and position according to the size of the device screen. This method is suitable for information-only websites, like e-newspapers and blogs, where there is no heavy interaction with the user. In fact, all websites built these days should be mobile-responsive, because a huge percentage of your visitors will be accessing the website via mobile devices, i.e. phones and tablets.

Mobi sites

In this approach, you build a separate version of your website specially designed for mobile devices, usually hosted in an *m.yourdomainname.com* site. Facebook follows this approach. You can go to facebook.com and m.facebook.com to compare the two websites. When you access facebook.com from your mobile device's browser, it automatically takes you to m.facebook.com

	Responsive website	**Mobi site**
Initial build cost	Higher	Lower
Access to information for users	All info on website is accessible on mobile deices	Only limited data is available on mobile devices
Ongoing maintenance requirements	Lower—only one code base and one content back-end to manage	Higher—two separate code bases and two separate content management back-ends
Search friendliness	Recommended by Google guidelines	Not recommended by Google guidelines
User experience	Typical top-to-bottom navigation. Not optimised for mobile devices	It can be optimised well for mobile device to provide a user experience similar to apps

Responsive websites and mobi sites are websites, often referred to as "web apps," which only work with an internet connection, using browsers like Chrome, Internet Explorer, and Safari on your mobile devices. Since they run in mobile browsers, they can't make full use of the mobile device's capabilities, such as accelerometer, contacts, camera, etc.

The term "Apps" is used to refer to mobile apps that are downloaded to the user's phone which can make use of all the capabilities of the mobile devices.

Two types of mobile apps

"Apps" generally used to refer to mobile apps, which are downloaded from Apple App Stores and Google Play Stores to various mobile devices (phones, tablets, etc.) run on the mobile device's operating system. There are two types of mobile apps: native and hybrid.

Native apps

Each mobile platform, like iOS, Android, and Windows, offers their own (native) software development kit (SDK), which has the tools and interfaces to build, run, and install their apps. For example, with Apple iOS, native apps are built using iOS system frameworks and objective-C language. Recently, Apple introduced Swift to build native iOS apps faster. Similarly, native Android apps are built using Java SDK. Native apps are installed physically on a device, and are therefore always available to the user, even when the device is in Airplane mode. Some data, however, may need online connectivity. Native apps provide the best user experience, since the user experience is customised for each platform. Since most features can be built without depending on internet connectivity, native apps are faster than web or hybrid apps. For example, the Angry Bird app, and many little game apps like it, are native apps. They can be used without any internet, whereas an app like Facebook needs internet connectivity to work.

Hybrid apps

Hybrid apps sit between web apps and native mobile apps. They mainly make use of web technologies to build the app, just as web apps do, but then they're wrapped inside a native app using web view. (Web view is basically a browser bundled inside a mobile application.)

Hybrid apps can make use of native UI elements. This allows hybrid apps to have significant cost savings, as the majority of the development is in web technologies and can be reused for all platforms, but at the same time they are downloadable on the App Stores like the native apps.

The disadvantage with hybrid apps is that they cannot provide a rich and dynamic user experience equivalent to native apps. Hybrid apps are slower than native apps, and most of the app features need internet connectivity to work. Game apps, for example, are best built as native apps, whereas simple business apps can be built as hybrid apps. Instagram is a hybrid app, for example. Though it uses a lot of native components and native UI elements, it uses a web view for the timeline feature.

Cross platform development

The other way to build apps cost effectively is by using cross platform development technology. Cross platform development uses tools and technology that allows developers to build apps for multiple platforms at the same time, instead of building one platform, like iOS or Android, at one time. You build the app once using the cross platform tool, and then simply publish the app in multiple platforms like iOS, Android, or Windows.

Sometimes people confuse cross platform development with hybrid apps. You can use cross platform technologies to build either native apps or hybrid apps.

For example, NativeScript and Xamarin are cross platform development technologies that allow you to build native apps for cross platforms.

Phonegap.com and Ionic Framework, for example, are cross platform technologies that allow you to build hybrid apps for multiple platforms.

Cross platform technology can often be a cheaper way to build apps, but it has technical limitations, especially in the area of UI. For example, they are not great for game apps or apps with sophisticated interactive reporting.

If you are feeling overwhelmed with all these technology terms being thrown at you, don't worry. All you need to understand to get started is that there is more than one way to skin a cat. Your developer must be able to discuss these options with you and recommend one over the other and why. Make sure this is part of the discussion with your developer.

Even if you are not a coder, having the basic technical knowledge discussed in this section and building on it will enable you to have meaningful technical discussions with your developer.

SECTION 4: HOW DO I FUND MY APP IDEA?

Do you need to raise funds for your app business? When is the right time to get funding? The sooner you raise funds, the more equity you have to give away in your app. Also, it is very hard to get investors when it is just an idea. When you have a working product, with data to show there is a demand for your product, you can raise funds without giving away as much of your equity.

14. Funding options for your app business

There are several key issues to explore before choosing your funding options. When app entrepreneurs start thinking about finding funding, three questions pop up right away:

- Should I raise funds for my idea, and if so, how much to raise and what do I give in return?
- When is the right time to get the funding for my app idea?
- What's the best way to find money?

The answer to these questions really depends on where you want to go with your idea and many of your personal preferences. Go back to your why. What is your live bigger category and what type of business do you want to create?

To raise or not to raise

If you want the app to provide you a good lifestyle with less working hours and steady cash flow, you're better off funding it yourself. Having investors means you become responsible for their money and need to provide answers to their questions. You may not have the same level of freedom and independent decision-making ability once you have external investors.

However, the biggest challenge I find with building an app business without any external funding is the "Acquire users first, make money later" approach taken by all funded startups. You will need to compete with other app businesses in the market who will spend significantly higher than you in marketing and also offer the app for free just to acquire users. For example, Uber with tens of millions of dollars in funding actually offered money to their customers (drivers) in many countries to use the app just to acquire the market share while they were losing a lot of money. They spent millions in marketing and user acquisition before they made a cent in profit. Can you imagine competing with Uber without any funding?

If you have huge vision for your app, want to take it global in a few years, it is quite impossible to do it without external funding.

Having said that **it is not impossible to create a successful app business without external funding.**

- *Markus Frind founded the dating site Plentyoffish in 2003, and built it to a very profitable company without any external funding. In 2015, he sold it to the Match group for $575,000,000 US in cash.*
- *Zoho is a very successful enterprise software company with hundreds of thousands of users which never took any external funding, and founder Sridhar Vembu shared he*

has no interest in funding (or an exit strategy), in spite of getting calls from investors every day.

So your personal preferences, your vision for the app, and the competition in your market plays a significant role in whether to raise funds or not.

Raising money: valuation

When you do decide to raise money from professional investors, your business valuation determines how much you can raise. **The value of your app business is based on two things. As a simple formula, it is directly proportional to the future potential of your business and inversely proportional to the risk in your business.** When you can demonstrate great future potential and low risks, your value goes up and you can raise good capital for a small equity. The most common method of valuating business is a multiple of revenue or profit. But for early stage app startups, there is often no revenue or profit. So the most common method of valuation for early stage app startups is either discounted cash flow method (DCF) or just an arbitrary value based on investment made in the app. In DCF method, you project the estimated profit for the next five or 10 years and discount it down to present value to determine the current value of your app business.

Based on one of these methods, if the value of your app business works out to be a million dollars, then, for example, you may choose to raise $100,000 from an investor and give away 10% equity in your app to the investor.

Finding money

There are four main professional funding sources for tech startups: crowdfunding, angel investors, venture funds, and "going public," or IPO. Let's look at each.

Crowdfunding

Crowdfunding is a way of attaining capital from a large pool of individual investors, friends, family, etc. This funding option also leverages the networks of these individual investors, increasing your reach exponentially. There is no limit on how much money you can raise using crowdfunding.

However, most crowdfunding platforms impose a time limit within which the target has to be achieved. Therefore, it is important to be reasonable with your funding goal. Also, running a crowdfunding campaign involves a learning curve and takes a lot of time, so be realistic about your funding goals.

There are two types of crowdfunding options available.

- In reward-based crowdfunding, entrepreneurs offer rewards that supporters/investors receive if the funding goal is attained, such as t-shirts, experiences, or the product itself when it's complete.
- In equity-based crowdfunding, entrepreneurs offer equity in exchange for capital if the funding goal is attained.

Some popular crowdfunding platforms include Kickstarter and Indiegogo. Popular crowdfunding platforms specialising in mobile apps include:

- Appsfunder.com
- Appbackr.com
- Appsplit.com
- Angel.co

Angel investors

Angel investors are wealthy individuals who invest in startups in exchange for equity in the startup company. These investors generally invest in the early stages of funding, providing seed funding anywhere from $25,000 to $1,500,000.

To look for potential angel investors, do an internet search for angel investors in your city. Don't write them a cold email; see if you can get an introduction from a mutual contact. Use LinkedIn to find out if you have a mutual contact and research the angel investors you'd like to target. Go to events they go to, network, and ask them out for a coffee.

For example, here are a few angel groups around Melbourne, Australia.

- https://www.australianinvestmentnetwork.com/business-proposal/industry-internet-ecommerceapps-7
- http://melbourneangels.net/
- https://angel.co/melbourne/investors
- http://businessangels.com.au/angels.php

Venture funds

Venture capital funds typically come into play after seed funding. Venture capitalists obtain funds from a plethora of sources, such as foundations, wealthy individual groups, endowment funds, etc. They invest much larger amounts than angel investors. Venture capital firms invest in established businesses, not ideas. They care about the ability to *execute*. So, get your idea built, acquire customers, create revenue, and *then* approach VC firms.

Below are some VC firms in Australia.

- Adventure Capital – http://adventurecapital.vc/
- BlackBird Ventures – http://blackbird.vc/
- OneVentures – http://www.one-ventures.com.au/
- Starfish Ventures – http://www.starfishvc.com/

IPO

IPO, or Initial Public Offering, is when your company shares are sold to the general public, usually with the help of an investment bank. Often, this is how the founders and investors get a return on their investment. A company selling common shares is never required to repay the capital to its public investors. The ability to quickly raise potentially large amounts of capital from the marketplace is one reason many companies go public. The disadvantages of going public are that the founders lose a lot of control over their own business, and are subject to much higher legal and other compliance requirements.

Some noteworthy Australian startups that went public include:

- *Atlassian. Started in 2002 in Sydney, Australia, with a $10,000 credit card, the founders say that the company has always been profitable. The company went public in December, 2015, selling 22,000,000 shares at $21 apiece, raking in $462,000,000 at a market valuation of nearly $4.4 billion.*
- *Rewardle. Founded in September 2011, founder Ruwan launched the platform in July 2012 and went public in just three years, in October 2014. The IPO raised $4,000,000, valuing the company at $30,000,000. It received a lot of criticism because it was too early and had only 64 paying customers at the time of IPO.*

Alibaba and Facebook are two of the biggest IPOs ever. In September 2014, Alibaba, the Chinese e-commerce company, went public in the US NASDAQ exchange at $21.8 billion, making it the biggest IPO ever at that time. When Facebook went public in May 2012, it raised $16 billion.

Fundraising is an essential skill for app entrepreneurs. Putting some time and research into fundraising from the start can help transform a great idea into a very successful business.

15. What are the different stages of funding an app startup?

Let's apply your understanding of the various types of fundraising and look at the different stages of funding many startups require and how much money they might seek at each stage. These include seed funding, at the very beginning, and "Series" funding.

Seed funding

Seed funds are raised during the early stages of a startup. Investors contribute a small amount of money to bring an idea to life. The immediate goal is to produce a Minimum Viable Product, or MVP.

Seed capital often comes from the company founders' personal assets, their friends and family, and sometimes from angel investors. Professional investors and banks see this as a very risky investment. If they do invest seed capital, professional investors may seek a considerable equity stake, as they are accepting a high amount of risk.

Seed funding is mainly used for preliminary market research and to develop the MVP. It may also be used for initial marketing of your product, to test your market and gain some traction.

Funding range: $50,000 – $1,000,000

- *Facebook's first ads in May 2004 generated about $2,400 in ad revenue that month. In June 2004, they raised a $500,000* *seed funding round at a $5,000,000 valuation from angel investor Peter Theil. Initially structured as a loan, the financing was later converted to a 10.2% equity stake in the company for Peter Theil.*

Series A funding

After you have a working product with a proven market and a revenue model, your series of VC funding starts. Series A funding is the first round of institutional venture capital funding. The name refers to the Series A preferred stock offered to the investors in exchange for their equity.

Typically, these funds are used for the first two years of operating costs, including software development, server maintenance, marketing/user acquisition, customer support, and other business operational costs.

Funding range: $2,000,000 to $10,000,000, in exchange for 10% – 30% stake of the company.

- In 2010, Airbnb raised $7,200,000 from Sequoia Capital and Greylock Partners. At that time, over 700,000 nights had been booked in more than 8,000 cities. The press release stated, "Airbnb will use their millions to continue global expansion, hire staff, make translated versions of the app, and create multiple payment options to suit any guest or host, no matter what country they're in."

Series B funding

The second round of major funding takes place after the company has proven success with Series A. In most cases, the company is already making decent revenue by this round.

Commonly, Series B funds are used to expand the team and build scale. It may include salaries, infrastructure costs such as server costs and office space, and/or the marketing and branding costs needed to enter a new region to achieve globalisation.

Funding range: $5,000,000 – $50,000,000

- *In 2013, Snapchat raised $80,000,000 in Series B funding led by venture firm IVP (Institutional Venture Partners).*

Series C funding

Series C funding is the third round of funding for companies which have already proved success in the market and have clear potential for a larger market. The purpose is to accelerate growth. Product diversification, acquisition, and tapping into the international markets are often the main focus points in Series C. Big banks, hedge funds, and public companies are involved at this stage, as the amounts can be in hundreds of millions of dollars.

Funding range: $100,000,000– $500,000,000

- *In 2013, Uber raised $258,000,000, led by Google ventures. This Series C funding put Uber at a post-money valuation of $3.7 billion.*

The funding amount and purpose of funding for each round shown above are approximations; it varies based on the company. The number of funding rounds are also not limited to Series A, B, and C; that depends on the growth of the organisation. *For instance, Pinterest, founded in 2009, has accumulated $1.3 billion in funding. Their latest round, in 2015, was a Series G, which raised $186,000,000.*

Fundraising histories of popular companies

Let's take a quick look at how some of the world's most popular companies raised money.

FACEBOOK		
Angel	$500,000	Peter Thiel Reid Hoffman
Series A	$12,700,000	Accel Partners
Series B	$27,500,000	Founders Fund Greylock Partners Meritech Capital Partners SV Angel
Series C	$240,000,000	Microsoft
Facebook had four rounds of Series C funding and accumulated over $200,000,000 in funding before going public.		

UBER		
Seed Funding	$200,000	Garrett Camp, founder Travis Kalanick, founder
Angel	$1,250,000	First Round
Series A	$11,000,000	Benchmark
Series B	$37,000,000	Manlo Ventures
Series C	$258,000,000	Google Ventures

Uber used several rounds of funding to sustain its expansion. The latest funding from Baidu garnered 1,200,000,000 US dollars in private equity, taking the total funding to over $10,000,000,000 by 2015, far exceeding the amounts raised by any company before in IPO.

AIRBNB		
Seed Funding	$620,000	Y Combinator Sequoia Capital
Series A	$7,200,000	Eight different Venture firms and investors
Series B	$112,000,000	Andreessen Horowitz
Series C	$200,000,000	Founders Fund

Airbnb saw more rounds of funding totalling $2.39 billion by 2015. The latest funding, by Firstmark Capital, accumulated $100,000,000 (private equity).

WHATSAPP		
Seed Funding	$250,000	Five friends of Brian Acton, co-founder of WhatsApp
Series A	$8,000,000	Sequoia Capital
Series B	$50,000,000	Sequoia Capital
WhatsApp did not have any more rounds of funding. However, on February 19th, 2014, Facebook acquired WhatsApp for a reported $19 billion.		

ATLASSIAN		
Seed Funding	A $10,000 credit card	Founders
Secondary market	$60,000,000	Accel Partners
Secondary market	$150,000,000	T. Rowe Price
Atlassian, founded in Sydney, Australia, raised $462,000,000 with its IPO on the US NASDAQ exchange.		

DROPBOX		
Seed Funding	$15,000 + $1,200,000	Y Combinator + seven investors
Series A	$6,000,000	Sequoia Capital
Series B	$250,000,000	Index Ventures
Series C	$350,000,000	BlackRock

SPOTIFY		
Series A	$21,640,000	Horizons Ventures Northzone Creandum Li Ka-Shing
Series B	$50,000,000	Wellington Partners Li Ka-Shing Horizons ventures
Series C	$12,598,180	Founders Fund (Sean Parker)
Series D	$100,000,000	Accel Partners Klieners Perkins Caufield & Byers DST Global
Spotify received further rounds of funding from investors. On June, 2015, Spotify received $526,000,000 from a total of 13 investors, taking its total funding to $1.06 billion.		

As you can see, these global app companies did not grow global because they are great ideas. The huge funding and support from the professional investors have helped them grow at such a large scale. So even if you think external funding is not for you, I recommend you prepare yourself for funding and stay open to the idea.

16. Top five things investors look for before investing in an early-stage tech startup

We've explored the different sources and stages of funding for app startups. There are not many other businesses in the world that can scale up as fast as app startups. When you are in the early stages and not making money from your app, getting investors is not easy. When you invite an investor to consider funding your app business, what criteria do they consider? Here are the top five we identified from our research and direct interviews with investors.

The "A" team

Investors truly believe in the saying, "Bet the jockey, not the horse." The majority of early-stage investors say they actually invest in the people backing the idea, rather than the idea itself. A skilful and passionate team with a proven track record will always have an edge over competitors who have a great idea but a sub-par team.

Questions investors ask themselves include, "Is the founder a doer or a dreamer? Are they determined and ready to put in the necessary work to build the business? Are they trustworthy? What is the team's track record?"

Market size

Venture capitalists and angel investors consider the size of the target market paramount. How big the company can grow depends on how big the market is for the product. To them, it doesn't matter how mind-blowing the idea is if the market isn't big enough. Most investors are looking for ideas that work across languages and cultures. Is your idea universal?

Clear business model

By looking at your business model (or business plan), investors can identify how well you have thought out and planned your business. They will look for how much the company can make in returns, and how soon, and what the exit strategy looks like. Competitor analysis, revenue model, customer segments, and distribution channels are a few key things that need to be included in your business model. Download our one-page lean business canvass template at appomate.com.au/resources

Risks

Investors take on considerable risk by investing in startups—especially early-stage startups. They want to know that the founding team or entrepreneur is aware of all the potential risks and has developed a risk-mitigation strategy to address these risks as they arise. When they ask you, "What are the risks involved in this business?" the last thing you want to say is that there are no risks. Make sure you perform risk analysis. The standard SWOT (Strengths/Weaknesses/Opportunities/Threats) analysis is one method to consider the risks and come up with mitigation plans.

Skin in the game

Investors look for proof that you strongly believe in your idea. Have you quit your job to get this business started? How much of your personal savings have you invested? Have you already made some progress with your idea by building the app or at least a prototype? Investors are more comfortable getting on a train that is already moving, rather than one that is just an idea.

Assess your app business by these five criteria. If you were an investor, how interested would you be in your own company? Remember that investors want maximum earning potential but minimum risks. That's what you are trying to communicate to the investors.

17. Creative ways to seed fund your app idea

Raising funds at the idea stage is completely different from raising funds for an app that is already successful. Professional investors aren't the only option to raise funds. Before you can bring on those big guns for funding, you need to prove you have something worth the investment. Let's explore some creative funding options for that early stage when you have a fantastic idea, but not much else.

Personal money, friends and family

The vast majority of apps are initially funded through the personal savings and resources of their founders (and the founders' friends and family). If you are not able to convince your friends and family to support your idea, it is going to be pretty hard to convince a stranger. Wouldn't you agree? The best part of this funding is often it is interest-free and you can negotiate good terms. If you are hesitant with this approach, is it because you probably don't believe in your idea fully? Look at it as sharing the opportunity with your friends and family. Be open and transparent. They might genuinely want to help you and take a small risk.

Crowdfunding

Crowdfunding is an option to raise funds for seed capital. Though most crowdfunding platforms adopt an "all or nothing" approach to crowdfunding campaigns, there are other options as well. For example, Indiegogo offers flexible plans which allow entrepreneurs to keep the money accumulated even if they don't reach funding goals.

Pitch contests

There are contests held around the world that allow people with ideas to get in front of investors and pitch their ideas. If you Google "pitch app ideas" or "startup pitching contest," you will find opportunities in your city. Many universities across the world also run contests to offer seed funding for startups.

- http://www.codelaunch.com/ is an annual event where people pitch their app ideas to a community of investors.
- http://sydstart.com/pitches/ is a startup conference in Sydney which runs pitching contests.
- There is even an app to pitch your app idea: http://thebigpitch.com.au/
- The University of Melbourne has its own startup incubator, called the Melbourne Accelerator Program. http://themap.co/
- Melbourne's RMIT University has an investment fund offering seed capital to students and alumni. http://www1.rmit.edu.au/students/neif

There are a lot of pitch deck templates available online. Sydney-based company Capital Pitch helps startups raise early stage venture capital and you can download their pitch deck template from their website at http://offers.capitalpitch. com/pitch-deck-download This pitch deck template is definitely one of the good ones out there.

Accelerators

Startup accelerators are programs that include education and mentorship for startup entrepreneurs with public pitch days.

Typically, accelerators invest $20,000 to $50,000, in exchange for equity.

Y-combinator and Techstars are among the first seed accelerators. Startmate and Angelcube are Australian-based accelerators.

Government grants

It is worthwhile to consider the many grants your government may offer for tech startups. In Australia, there is a research and development program that provides a significant tax incentive to app companies that qualify.

The R&D tax incentive program helps you get up to 45% of your research and development expenses back when you are in a loss position, or provides a tax offset of up to 45% when you are in a profit position. Your app idea must be novel and qualify as a research and development project.

- https://www.ato.gov.au/Business/Research-and-development-tax-incentive/About-the-program/

There are many companies and tax agents which help you apply for this R&D tax incentive program.

The Victorian Government in particular supports innovation by providing funding to entrepreneurs who focus on projects that simplify policy changes and aim at providing value to the public.

- http://www.vic.gov.au/publicsectorinnovation

The city of Melbourne offers grants to small businesses and startups.

- https://www.melbourne.vic.gov.au/SiteCollection Documents/small-business-grants-guidelines-2015. pdf

The Australian Government also provides financial assistance by funding new businesses.

- http://australianbusinessgrants.com.au/new-business-startup/

The Australian Government has an Entrepreneurs' Programme for budding entrepreneurs.

- http://www.business.gov.au/advice-and-support/EIP/Pages/default.aspx

The Queensland Government-funded "iLab" is one of Australia's largest schemes for technology startups, and has incubated over 100 startups.

- http://www.ilabaccelerator.com/

The Western Australian Government offers an "Innovator of the Year Award," granting the winner a $100,000 package.

- http://www.commerce.wa.gov.au/ScienceInnovation/Innovator/about.htm

Check which funding programs you qualify for by answering a few questions at the following link.

- http://www.australiangovernmentgrants.org/blog/?s=grants+young+entrepreneurs+Melbourne

Startup funding loans

Many organisations offer loans to startups and other small businesses. These funds can be utilised by businesses as seed or growth money.

Some good sources are:

- Kikka Capital makes things easier for businesses by providing approval for a business loan of up to $100,000 in just seven minutes. https://www.kikka.com.au/
- MoneyPlace specialises in peer-to-peer lending with funding up to $35,000. https://moneyplace.com.au/
- Moula offers funding to startups and provides an option of instant approval for funding of up to $100,000. https://moula.com.au/

If you Google "startup loans" you will find a lot of options.

Personal funding, crowdfunding, pitch contests, accelerators, government grants, and startup loans all represent valid avenues to raising the funds you need in the early days. Don't believe you can't find the money to pursue your great idea!

SECTION 5: HOW DO I DEVELOP MY IDEA INTO AN APP?

18. Five approaches to getting started

In the current app-economy, where everyone either has or is developing an app that is "the next BIG THING," it is helpful to understand some of the most common ways to get started on the journey. The following are five different approaches to getting your app idea kick-started.

Learn to code

Yes, you heard it right! Learn the art of coding through platforms like Udemy or Codecademy, and get started with your relatively simple app idea. This is a time-consuming method ideal for those with much time on their hands, but no funds. It can take anywhere from three years to 10 years to become reasonably good at coding and able to create a good app on your own.

Explore the DIY platforms

Are you looking to build a simple app with no sophisticated features, but don't want to learn hardcore coding and are hindered by a lack of investment? Do-it-yourself app-building tools like Appmakr, Appsme, and AppInventor may just be the right thing for you. These tools make use of pre-built templates to quickly and easily create your app. Even better, many of them don't even charge for using the service.

Build a virtual team

In this scenario, you build your team of developers, architects, UX designers, and testers through outsource platforms. A number of websites like Upwork.com, Freelancer.com, and Guru.com provide easy access to a large pool of app developers from across the world. Cloudpeeps.com is a good one to find a higher-quality digital team. There is an obvious cost advantage to this approach. However, you had better be a good project manager as the buck stops with you. Coordinating people around the world will take more time and effort than you might originally think—especially if this is your first time doing it.

BYOT: build your own team

If you are really confident about the success potential of your app idea—say you're convinced you have the next Uber or Airbnb—and you have secured some good funding, you may build up your own development team and management structure. This approach is typically for those who have been down this path before building successful businesses, are funded, or know how to raise millions in investment. This approach is probably the most expensive but the quickest and where you have the most control. You can also find good programmers who will build the app for an equity in your business. It is not easy though as good programmers often either work on their own idea or get paid really well by tech companies. This is another example where your sales skill can help to sell the value of your app and have someone to quit their job to join you as a partner to build your idea.

Find a development agency

An experienced app development firm can act as your development partner to help you get your app from the idea stage to the profitability stage. Entrepreneurs looking for holistic support must perform due diligence before partnering with an app development firm to obtain the highest level of quality, reliability, and promptness. This approach is for entrepreneurs who have a budget to get the project off the ground, and typically well suited to those who are running another business or performing a "day job" while the app development is happening in parallel.

Ultimately, the best app kick-starter approach depends really on the resources you have—time, skills, and money, and how advanced your app is. Building your own team or using a reputable development partner increases your chances of success. Although virtual teams and freelancers may work out as a cheaper option, I am yet to find any success stories using those approaches.

19. Manage your costs well

Poor budgeting and underestimated forecast of expenses is one of the common reasons many app businesses cannot continue to operate. Success is about understanding and managing numbers. You need to be aware of all the expenses your app business will incur, so you can forecast expenses and keep things in control.

In this chapter, you will learn the different costs involved in the initial startup phase to get your app to the market. It will help you make informed buying decisions when you are building your app.

The key expense categories in the startup phase include:

Building the app:

1. Branding
2. UI/UX design
3. Development
4. Testing

(Your version one goes live after development and testing)

Keeping the app alive:

5. Software and subscription fees
6. Hosting
7. Maintenance of the app
8. App improvements
9. Customer support
10. Marketing

Costs involved in app development

Marketing costs

With hundreds and thousands of apps clamouring for users' attention, it is important to have a reasonably good branding for your app. Branding includes your domain name, logo, tag line, website set-up, social media handles set-up, and a brand style guide for your app business.

On average, startup businesses spend a few thousand on initial branding. Best practice is to start with something simple and not too expensive. Logo competition sites (like 99designs. com) are a really great way to get nice logos and designs done for few hundred dollars.

Similarly, companies generally do not spend a lot on domain names initially. Uber had ubercab.com before it acquired uber.com. Twitter was twittr.com for many years before it had the money to buy twitter.com. Companies have spent millions of dollars on domain names when the time is right.

To get started, all you need is a domain name that is unique and has all or most social media handles available. http://knowem.com/ is a great site to search and secure a good brand name.

The recommended startup budget for basic branding including domain name, logo, style guide, and social media pages is approximately $5000.

Design costs

Design costs largely involve the User Interface and User Experience of an app. UI/UX is how the user interacts with your app to access every feature and functionality of your app. Good UX design is critical to the success of your app. Most importantly, apps need to be intuitive. You cannot leave it to the developers or traditional graphic designers to decide the flow, design, look, and feel of your app. There are specialised mobile app UX experts who live and breathe app UI/UX design. You should allocate budget for a UX expert's time. UI/UX cost depends how rich you want the UI to be (animations, special effects, etc.) and how many screens there are in your app. These variables determine how much time the UX expert needs to spend on your app.

The recommended startup/MVP budget for UI/UX is $2000 to $20,000, depending on the number of screens in your app. Based on my experience, an MVP app may have from 10 screens to 100 screens.

Development costs

This involves paying programmers for the actual coding of the app. This is where the majority of the time is spent in building apps. Most apps built these days need to work on multiple platforms and require a web back-end. This means you need at least three different developers—iOS, Android, and web. Developers who can code both front-end and back-end (full stack developers) are scarce and cost significantly more than average developers.

The development time required depends on the size and complexity of the app. Here are some questions that will help you evaluate your app.

- How many platforms will the app work on? (iPhone, Android, Windows, mobile website)
- How many screens are there in your app?
- How big is the features list and how advanced are the features? As a novice in app development, you may not be able to understand if a feature you request is advanced or basic. The best way to validate that is to talk to more than one developer.
- How many user types interact with the app and the system? For example, compare WhatsApp, where you have just one type of user, versus Uber, where you have two: drivers and passengers. The functional requirements are different for each user. Many apps also need an admin/moderator user to monitor and moderate usage of the system. For example, YouTube has features for content moderators who check for piracy and adult rating of uploaded content and they block the content and users who violate the terms.
- How much integration is required with device features like GPS, cameras, accelerometers, etc.?
- How much integration (API) is required with third-

party systems? The app complexity and cost increases significantly when you have third-party integrations, like payment gateways, transactional email systems, or other internal systems.

The recommended startup budget for initial MVP development is $10,000 to $100,000, based on size and complexity of the app.

Testing costs

Developers typically use simulators in their computers to test the features they have built for mobile phones. Testing iPhone apps (as of Dec 2016), you have iPhone 5, 5s, 6, 6 plus, 6s, 7. You have iOS versions 7, 8, 9, 10. You need testers to test the app in these different combinations, because the app working fine in one device/OS version does not guarantee proper functioning in all the other devices/OS versions. At a minimum, test the app for the latest two versions of OS and phone models for each platform.

The recommended startup testing budget is 30% of your development costs.

Professional app development firms also have business analysts and product managers to manage requirements and coordinate the work among the team of UI/UX designers, developers, and testers.

As you can see, the bulk of expenses around developing your app relates to paying for people's time for the various skills you need to leverage to create your app. If you learn and become an expert in one or more of these skills, you may be able to save some costs.

Cost to build world's best startups

Nextweb (in 2013) released how much it would cost to build the world's hottest startups, based on its interview with some agencies and developers based in the US.

App	Cost
Twitter	$50,000 to $250,000
Instagram	$100,000 to $300,000
WhatsApp	$120,000 to $250,000
Uber	$1,000,000 to $1,500,000
Facebook	$500,000 plus
Shopify	$250,000 to $300,000

Keep in mind, the numbers here are based on a fixed set of features taken from a completed app—but this is never the case when you build an app from scratch. You will add, remove, and change many features as you go. When Instagram initially launched, it was quite different to the Instagram now. So, the actual total cost to get to where they are now would be much higher than what is listed by Nextweb, due to all the changes they performed along the way.

Expenses after launching your app

Software and subscription fees

Once the app is developed, you will need various services to keep it running.

- A developer account currently costs $99/year with Apple and $25 with Google Play Store. You need this account to submit your app to the App Store and Google Play.

- App Store and Google Play take their 30% cut on any app sales and in-app purchases and only pay the remaining 70% to you.
- Payment gateway commission. If your app is using a payment gateway, like PayPal or Stripe, to accept payments, they charge a percentage of each transaction plus a fixed transaction fee.
- Third-party software licences, like push notification services, analytics software, and customer support software are typically free up to a certain number of users. Once you exceed the user threshold, you may incur monthly charges.

Hosting

Most apps require a back-end cloud server to store the data and allow users to access the app data regardless of the device they use. Amazon web services, Microsoft Azure, and Google Cloud are popular cloud services. Your server hosting costs can be as little as $100 a month, but will fluctuate based on these variables:

- Data storage
- Amount of data exchange—download and upload to server
- Computation power required by your app

For example, Instagram, which stores billions of pictures with image filtering and processing features, requires not only huge data storage but also considerable computing power from the server.

When Facebook originally launched, the initial server cost was $85 a month. By 2012, Facebook had more than 800 million users and was serving 300M photos per day; it spent $860M to host and serve the data – around $1 per active user. According to their SEC documents, their annual hosting costs were $0.60 per user in 2011 and $0.40 in 2010.

Twitter spent nearly $130M on hosting costs in 2012, or about $0.70 per user.

App maintenance—bug fixing and support

The operating system of mobile devices, and mobile device models themselves, constantly change. Apple provides major updates to their iOS approximately once a year, and releases a new model of their phone every year. The App Store also changes the development environment. For example, in early 2015, Apple made it mandatory that all apps need to have 64-bit support, as it introduced 64-bit architecture A7 chip in iPhone 5s to increase their phones' speed. In December 2015, it updated its programming language from Objective-C to Swift. All of this impacts your app, and therefore, planning for app maintenance expenses is a must to keep your app relevant through time.

The cost of app maintenance also depends on how quickly you introduce new features. The competitive nature of your market, as well as your usage data and user feedback, will inform what improvements you should make. For example, accounting apps like Xero constantly introduce new features, as the space is getting very competitive. On average, they release a new set of features to their app every two weeks. Maintenance costs are typically high for subscription-fee-based apps and revenue sharing apps. As customers pay an ongoing fee, they expect an ongoing service.

Marketing

Your marketing and distribution costs, like online marketing, Google ads, Facebook ads, or TV ads, all depend on your marketing goals and corresponding budget. The cost to acquire one user, known as CPA (Cost Per Acquisition), often decides the success or failure of an app. In a growth hacking conference in Silicon Valley, I learned Dropbox when they first launched was spending $200 to $300 in Google AdWords to acquire one customer who pays only $60/year.

When people come up with app ideas, they often assume they just need to build the app and users will come, so they forget to allocate any budget towards marketing. Unfortunately, that's not the case, as there are millions of apps available in the app stores shouting for customer attention. You will learn various methods of marketing in the marketing chapter. Make sure you plan and allocate a budget towards marketing. You need at least tens of thousands of dollars to do some initial marketing to acquire your first few thousand users. Building the app is probably the easiest part of creating your app business. Initial marketing to get enough people to hear about your app and make them not just download but use your app regularly is probably one of the most difficult stages in your app business journey.

Customer support

As you acquire users, you'll need a customer support team to handle customer requests. You want positive reviews and ratings in the App Store or Google Play. You want the customer to contact you directly when there is a problem, instead of complaining or posting negative reviews on app stores or social media. This means you may need to spend your time supporting the customers, or employing a customer support person, to respond to customer requests and queries. There are special customer support software, like Zendesk and Freshdesk, to track and resolve customer support requests and live chat systems like BoldChat and MyLiveChat, which enable you to respond to your customer queries in real time. You may not incur a huge customer support cost during the early days when you don't have many users, but successful app businesses have a full-time customer support team or customer success team whose job is to handle customer queries and complaints.

20. Building a quality app

Whatever method you decide to use to build your app, it's paramount that your end product has great quality. With millions of apps available, users have no time for apps that are not intuitive or are riddled with defects that reduce their experience. **With apps available for everything you can imagine, what differentiates your app more is not what your app can *do*, but how reliable, easy, and engaging your app is.**

Great quality apps can get you featured on the App Store and Google Play, which will help you grow faster. This chapter will educate you on different factors that contribute towards the quality of the app and what steps you can take to ensure the quality of your app when you build yours.

Quality of UI design

Everything else being constant, a user prefers a product that looks and feels good. I'm not intending to teach you UI design here but empower you to see the differences in quality so you can make the right decisions. A good UI design starts with consistency.

- Is everything like fonts, colours, layouts, and position and placement of different elements consistent across your app?

- Do you have a style guide to navigate your design decisions and ensure consistency?
- Are high quality images used everywhere?
- Do all the fonts/words look sharp and not blurry?
- Are you following Apple, Google design guidelines?

The App Store and Google Play have their own detailed design guidelines and recommendations for inclusion. Learn these guidelines and follow them to improve your app quality and also your chances of getting featured in the app stores.

Apple Store UI guidelines

https://developer.apple.com/ios/human-interface-guidelines/overview/design-principles/

Android UI design guidelines

https://developer.android.com/guide/practices/ui_guidelines/index.html

Quality of UX design

UX design is about consciously designing the experience of the user while using your app.

- Is your app intuitive, so the user can quickly and simply learn how to use the app without huge amounts of training?
- Is your app easy to use, so users can do what they want quickly without too many taps and steps to accomplish a particular task?
- Does your app engage the user and make the user want to explore different features of the app?

One of the common problems I see is when traditional web and graphic designers get into mobile UX design and design for mobile apps. They simply design how they would design for the web/desktop and shrink the size to fit the smaller, mobile screen. But this does not work because web/desktop design is based on interaction with a keyboard and mouse whereas mobile app interactions are with users' fingers. Also, there are many other mobile device specific user interactions which are very different to a website design, for example, a swipe instead of a <Next> button. The best approach to design your mobile app is to engage a mobile UX design specialist.

UX design is often the difference between successful and unsuccessful apps. Users usually have access to several apps for any one purpose, and will give multiple apps a try before deciding which one they want to use and which ones to delete. Quettra, a mobile intelligence startup, found that the average app loses 77% of its users within three days of installation and the main reason is use.

Quality of functions

The functional quality of your app relies primarily on how well the developer understands the app requirements and, after being fully developed, how well the app is tested.

With a myriad of mobile devices, operating systems, and browsers, the app must be tested in multiple environments to ensure functional quality. Make a list of popular browsers, devices, and operating systems you want to test your app for, and make sure your test team addresses all of them. When you engage a developer, ask them what devices, operating systems, and browsers they will test your app for and how.

Poor functional quality shows up as bugs. A good developer develops the app right the first time, requiring very low testing efforts. The basic types of testing to ensure functional quality include the following:

Unit testing. Your app code is made up of small units, or components related to specific features of your app. For example, a feature to integrate with the GPS to track location could be a unit within your app's code that needs to be tested individually. The developer will continually test these small units within your app to ensure each unit works as intended.

Integration testing. This is to test an entire subsystem, ensuring that the whole set of units play nicely together.

Functional testing. Here the end-to-end scenario of your app is tested by your test team according to the documented functional requirements of your app.

The unit testing, integration and functional testing are performed by your app developers/testers at different stages of your app development and when the app is ready, the team provides the app for your testing and approval.

User acceptance testing. When your development team reports your app is working as per expected functional requirements, you can have a group of end users, friends, family, colleagues, potential users actually use the app and provide feedback on their experience with the app. This is a critical phase of your development. Based on the feedback you get, you may choose to fix/update the app or go live.

Though a lot of app startups test the app manually, you should also make use of *automated testing*, particularly if your app is large and complex. One of the big challenges with app development is when you make a small change or update to one part of the app, it affects other parts of the app which were previously developed. In order to handle this, testers perform regression testing to verify the software previously developed and tested still functions correctly after some changes or updates are made to the software. When the app is large and complex, it means that you may spend only a few hours to do an update to the app but a few days to test the entire app again. This will slow down your app creation process. There are a number of tools and services available for testing automation. Some of the popular ones are selenium, appium.io, and Telerik. Using these tools, testers write testing scenarios and the tools test the software automatically instead of human testers spending days testing every time you make an update to your app.

With proper requirement documentation and a good development/testing team equipped with appropriate testing tools and practices, you can ensure the functional quality of your app is great.

Quality of performance

The robustness, performance, and maintainability of your app depends on the structural quality of your code. Structural quality includes how well the architecture of the entire software is designed and how modularised and structured the code is.

Poor structural quality—usually the result of too many shortcuts to save time and money—can have a negative impact on the cost and time required to maintain your app in the future. This is where the balance between designing and building robust code needs to be balanced with the Minimum Viable Product concept. There are trade-offs as you shift your app from the MVP to a more stable and scalable app. It may not be a big problem when your app is initially launched (or it may), but as you proceed with future updates, enhancements, and general maintenance to the app, bad structural quality may show up in following ways:

- Inconsistent app bugs—certain bugs are hard to reproduce in any given scenario; the bug appears random.

- Bug dominoes—fixing one bug leads to the creation of one or more bugs.
- Big effort for small change—small changes take a long time to implement because the app's foundation is unsteady and hard to debug.
- App crashes—the app often crashes, shuts itself down, or throws you out of the app for no known reason.
- App responsiveness—the app is often unresponsive when loading, or very slow when certain features are used.

These issues often arise (not always) because the developer hasn't followed proper coding standards/framework and good app architecture. In these instances, there may be little code documentation or code structure to identify different elements of the code and fix the issue. It makes it very difficult for a new developer to understand and support your app.

So how do you assess the code quality of your developer to ensure a solid foundation?

- Download and use the app they have developed.
- Talk to their clients. Ask them if they experienced the symptoms of bad code (described above) while they worked with the developer you are assessing.
- Have a look at the code of their past work. A good code would look neat, like a nicely formatted Word document, versus a Word document with poor formatting and text all over the place. You would be able to see English comments in different places explaining the functions, code, and the changes made, white space, and meaningful names used for variables.
- Ask the developer what framework and architecture they use in their coding. Ask them what tools they use and how they maintain the code versions.

While you can do load testing and performance testing to test the robustness, performance, and structural quality of your app, the only way to ensure structural quality is to have good, experienced developers in your team.

When you have validated the following quality components, you can be confident your app is good.

- Quality of the graphics/UI design—How does the app look and feel?
- Quality of the user experience/UX design—How easy, intuitive, and engaging is it to use the app?
- Quality of the functions—How well are the app features designed and developed, and do they work as expected?
- Quality of performance—How robust is the app? Do the app images, pages, and features load fast? Does the app crash?

21. Deliver your app on time

When you start on your app journey, you may have a certain compelling event coming up like a conference, expo, or a festival season by when you may wish to have your app ready. It is important you understand that it not easy to finish a software project by a planned timeline due to a number of reasons inherent to software development. However, having the right knowledge can help you avoid the common factors leading to project delay. In this chapter, you will learn the most common challenges to on-time app development, and how you can avoid them.

Problem: Scope creep. App requirements are analysed and documented during the requirement phase. Changes in features and functionality are inevitable; however, they must be properly managed in an effective product release plan in order to avoid delays of the original requirement.

Solution: Prioritise your requirements and decide on what features will be included in each stage. Develop the discipline to put new ideas into a wish list for future phases of development.

Problem: Gold plating. One or more of the team members (including you) get too stuck on minute details irrelevant to the end user.

Solution: Don't be a perfectionist. It is important to adhere to the 80/20 rule. And when we say 80/20, we mean 20% of what you focus on will deliver 80% of the value, so make sure you are focusing in the areas most important to your potential market. Quality is important, but things like moving a button two pixels to the right should not stop you from going live. Lock in a go-live date that everyone works towards. Get your first version out and enhance your app as you go.

Problem: Overly optimistic schedules. To win your work, some developers may agree to overly optimistic timelines. In the end, it only leads to buggy software and further delays.

Solution: Work with an app developer with a proven track record of finishing projects on time. Establish and agree on a project timeline before the project begins. Add contingencies to project deadlines. Work with a professional app development company that can provide you with customer references about the quality and timeliness of their delivery.

Problem: Complexity/capability fit. If your app is complex and the development team lacks the breadth and depth of technical capability required, the team won't be able to estimate the effort to deliver your app accurately, and your schedule will suffer.

Solution: Only a professional and experienced team can build a complex app, so make sure they've successfully accomplished projects with similar technical requirements to your own. Choose a development team based on the complexity of your app. To be able to do this well, you need to have a good appreciation of the level of complexity of what you are trying to create.

Problem: Perform your role. It is not uncommon for the app entrepreneurs to think that their job is over once they explain their idea to the development team. There are many areas that need your involvement, like performing reviews and providing regular feedback to ensure what is being built is what you have asked for. If you are not diligent with this, a small misunderstanding can lead to weeks or months of rework and the project schedule can slip easily.

Solution: Commit time to work with your development team. Your active participation is crucial for success. Read more in the coming sections regarding your responsibility during different stages of development.

Problem: Requirements are not analysed and documented properly. Developers build what is specified in the use case or requirements document. Gaps in expressing initial requirements lead to confusion during the design and development phase.

Solution: Carefully analyse and document the app requirements *before* the development (iteration) begins. Read the documentation more than once to ensure everything you want in your app is captured correctly and completely.

Problem: Apple review rejections. Apple is quite strict when it comes to App Store submission guidelines. Apple review guidelines are also not very black and white. There are some grey areas, and Apple may reject your app submission for completely unexpected reasons and request changes to be made in your app.

Solution: Ensure you follow App Store guidelines clearly before submitting the app. It is important to understand the guidelines before building your app so you don't end up building an app that Apple will never approve. Experienced developers would know what would clearly not be accepted by Apple. For example, to avoid the 30% commission to Apple, app entrepreneurs may ask the developers to redirect the payment page to their website so users pay via the website instead of the app. From experience, I know Apple will reject the app during review and will ask you to remove the website redirection feature in the app. There are many other such possible scenarios for rejection. So schedule time in your project plan to allow for potential changes during the App Store review process.

So in section 5, you learned the different approaches to building your app, understanding and managing your costs while building your app, and ways to ensure quality and on-time delivery of your app. In the next section, you will learn some strategies and tactics to promote your app after you have built it.

SECTION 6: HOW DO I PROMOTE MY APP?

22. The number-one way to maximise your app downloads

You had a fantastic idea for an app. Unlike thousands of others who only dream, you made it happen. You believed in your idea, found the money, found the right team, and created your app. Your app is live. It works, and it works well! Those are all major achievements … but they mean nothing unless people download and use your app, hopefully generating income for you in the process! So how do you get people to know about your app, download it, and use it when millions of apps are fighting for their attention? In this section, you will learn exactly that.

How do users discover the apps they use? Tech Crunch reported, "On iOS, 47% said they found the app through the App Store's search engine, while 53% of Android users did the same on Google Play."

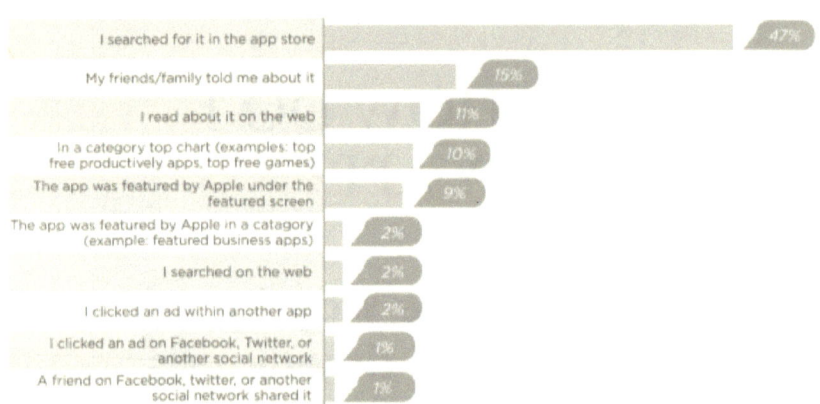

This makes sense. Each store offers about 1.5 million apps, so browsing isn't realistic. Users search for what they want and explore downwards the top entries of their search results.

How can you leverage this knowledge to maximise your downloads?

The answer is App Store optimisation: the process that gets your app to the top of the search results, increasing the number of visits to your app page, and thus the number of downloads. You have seven big chances to position your app for success through App Store optimisation.

Steps to App Store optimisation

Title

The title, or name, of your app is very important. Along with your app name, include relevant keywords in your title, so your app comes up on search results for those keywords.

Example: Shoebox is a photo backup app. Its full title in the App Store is *"Shoebox—photo backup cloud."* When you search for "photo backup app" Shoebox comes up as second result—even before the Google photos app—because it has the words "photo backup" in its title.

Keywords

When you submit your app to the App Store, you can list keywords for it. Think about specific words your audience will use in searching for this type of app, and then separate each word with commas. Keywords are limited to 100 characters total, so avoid repetition and plurals.

Potential users of "Shoebox photo backup" may use search terms like "photo backup app," "photo cloud storage app," or "free photos backup apps" to search for an app when they are looking to back up their photos. So you would use the following keywords if you were submitting this app: photo, cloud, backup, storage, free.

Description

Describe your app in a concise and engaging manner that grabs the attention of your audience. Explain its features and functions, and what makes the app unique and different from other apps. The first few sentences are most important, because a limited number of words show up before the user must click "more." This number of words is shorter for phones compared to the display on tablets and computers. Use some of your important keywords in the description, but avoid overusing them.

Categories

The primary category you select will be the category in which the app appears for search results and in the "Explore" section of the App Store. Be sure to select the category that best describes the main function of your app.

The Shoebox app best fits in the photos and videos category. This category, as defined by Apple, includes "Apps that assist in capturing, editing, managing, storing, or sharing photos and videos." Read the description of the category provided by Apple to be sure your app fits the category.

Screenshots and app preview

Images speak more loudly than words. Use screen shots that really communicate the benefits of your app. The App Store also allows you to submit a short video (15 to 30 seconds) of your app to demonstrate the features and functions. This can really differentiate your app from other search results and you can also use the video for different marketing purposes like in Facebook paid ads.

App icon

Your app's icon may be the first thing users notice when they see the app in a search result. It creates a first impression of your app. If the app icon, screen shots, and video are not of really high quality and good resolution, users subconsciously make judgements about the quality of your app.

User ratings and reviews

The App Store gives preference to apps with higher ratings and number of reviews. Encourage your users to rate and review your app. You can use tools like Apptentive to enable in-app ratings and reviews. Apptentive allows users to submit the review to the App Store while they are using your app without leaving your app.

There are plenty of sources online regarding App Store optimisation. Go straight to the source to get the right education.

https://developer.apple.com/app-store/product-page/

https://developer.apple.com/library/ios/documentation/ LanguagesUtilities/Conceptual/iTunesConnect_Guide/ Chapters/FirstSteps.html

23. Quickest way to get started with your app promotion

There are many, many ways to promote your new app. App Store optimisation requires only learning and testing. Most promotional techniques like word-of-mouth referral and procuring strategic partnerships and celebrity endorsement take research, networking, and building relationships. They take time.

One very quick and direct method of promotion is to use ad platforms and networks to pay for strategically placed ads online to direct people to your App Store page or website.

There are different types of paid advertisement campaigns you can run online, placing ads on websites, social media, and other apps where your target market is active. This is done with the help of an ad network that connects the advertisers and publishers.

Different types of paid ads

Pay per click

The most popular type of paid ads is pay per click (PPC). In this method, you pay your ad publisher for every click your ad receives. Google search ads are the most popular, but also the most expensive, when it comes to PPC ads. Facebook, Twitter, and Instagram all offer their own advertisement services. In late 2016, Apple released App Store search ads (only in the US) to help app developers promote apps on App Store.

The cost per click (CPC) for the PPC ads can range from a few cents to a few dollars, based on the competition and the platform. For example, to advertise an accounting app can cost up to $20 per click on Google. Facebook ads are much cheaper than Google AdWords. You can display banner advertisements in Facebook for 10 to 20 cents per click. But this is going up as more people start using the Facebook ad platform.

Pay per install

The other type of ads popular in the app space is the pay per install, or PPI, ads. Here you place your digital ad in different media, and are charged only when your app is installed. There are not many ad networks which offer ads on a cost per install basis. Currently, Appnext, Flurry (recently acquired by Yahoo), and Jampp are a few popular ad networks that provide ads on a cost per install basis. They require your app to be a free app or at least have a free version to be able to create PPI ads.

Cost per million

The third most popular ad option these days is the cost per million (CPM) impressions, where you pay the ad network for every million views of your ad. It is hard to measure return on investment with this method, but it is often cheap, and works well to create awareness of your brand. Most ad networks, including Facebook and Google, offer options for advertisers to pay on a CPM basis.

The best part about these digital ads, as compared to traditional ads like TV or radio, is that you can place the ads on your target users' mobile devices. They are already seeing your app advertisement in their iOS or Android device, and it only takes one click to go to your App Store page to download and start using your app.

Whether you use CPC, CPI, or CPM, you can display your ads in different formats in the desktop and mobile devices.

Different ad formats

Search ads

These are text-based ads that appear in your search results when you search for a keyword in Google, Yahoo, Bing, and other search engines. Typically, they have character limits of up to 150 characters.

Banner ads

This is the most popular format, where your ad appears on the top or bottom of the screen with relevant text and graphics. AdMob research shows the majority of mobile app users prefer banner ads to be placed at the top of the screen. It is less intrusive compared to other formats, but the small size limits the amount of information you can include in these ads.

Native ads

These are ads that integrate seamlessly with the look and feel of the app in which the ads are published. For example, in Facebook you can promote your newsfeed. Though it is a paid advertisement, it looks like a normal newsfeed to the audience.

Interstitial ads

These are ads that display across the entire screen—often when users open or close an app in which your ad is placed. The large size of this ad type allows you to display more information, with a clear call to action. It often earns higher engagement than the other ad types.

Rich media and video ads

These are dynamic ads which can include animation, interaction with the user, videos, etc. They require a substantial budget to create, but offer a higher engagement and conversion than other ads.

This is one of my favourite video ads for an app by Chatbooks app.

https://www.youtube.com/watch?v=PTTs7ewuDY8

Conclusion

You can create all these different ad formats within CPC, CPI, and CPM methods, in a variety of ad networks. The only certain way to find which options are best for your app is to try a combination of different options, and calculate your CPA (cost per user acquisition) for each option.

Advertising is a very quick and efficient method of promotion, but it takes some money, and trial and error to employ it most effectively. For many apps, however, it is an essential leg of the marketing plan.

Below are links to set up advertisements in Google, Facebook, Twitter, and Instagram.

- http://www.google.com.au/adword
- https://developers.facebook.com/docs/app-ads
- https://business.twitter.com/solutions/drive-app-installations-or-engagements
- https://business.instagram.com/advertising

Here are links to some mobile-specific ad networks. You can Google "mobile ad network" and find lots of them.

- http://www.startapp.com/
- https://www.google.com/admob/
- http://www.media.net/
- https://www.leadbolt.com/

24. How to get famous people to make your app famous

We saw how App Store optimisation and paid ads can help promote your app. Another way to make a big splash is to have celebrities and social media influencers help bring awareness to your product and brand.

Why are celebrities/influencers valuable to you?

Celebrities and other influencers with a huge following have the power to promote based on their exposure, popularity, mission, and values. Whether or not people like them, they get attention, and so your app will, too. They often have a variety of avenues to get their message out, from TV interviews to blogs and social media pages. For better or worse, many people trust celebrities, and the products they promote benefit from generalised trust.

These celebrated people do not necessarily have to be globally known or have millions of followers and fans. Someone with thousands of followers can still add great value to your app promotion.

Why would a celebrity or social media influencer promote your app?

You may wonder why a celebrity might want to talk about your product to their fans. If your app is really valuable to their followers, they will consider talking about it for one or more of these reasons.

It might simply be because they get paid, or get a commission from the sale of the products they talk about. But often, it's also because they want to share useful and cool stuff with their fans and followers. They want to engage and give value to their fans as often as they can. They want their fans to share their posts with their friends in order to create more fans. Many successful people just want to help others to be successful. Don't assume people want to help only if they get some personal benefits out of it. Maybe the sense of fulfilment and gratification from helping others is all they want. So ask. If you are not good at asking, check out the book *The Aladdin Factor* by Jack Canfield on the topic of asking. It's a great read.

How do you identify influencers who will promote your app?

Google Alerts is a great tool. You can set up alerts on topics relevant to your product, and see who's talking about them, and where.

AuthoritySpy is a great tool to search and find authorities and influencers in your industry. Klout is another tool where you can find social media influencers and it even ranks them based on their social influence.

There are many other online tools to help you identify influencers. I encourage you to use the mother of all online tools, Google, and simply search "websites to find influencers."

How to approach them?

Using the above methods, you search and identify a list of celebrities and influencers who have access to your target market. Now you have to approach them and there are a number of ways you can do it.

Paid

If you are well funded, you may have the budget to pay the celebrity directly or hire a professional agency to make a deal happen for you. Getting a celebrity with millions of followers to promote your app is not cheap. For example, big brands reportedly shell out $100,000 to $300,000 for a single Instagram post by Kylie Jenner who has over 90 million followers on Instagram. You can also find influencers with a few thousand followers who may charge only a few hundred dollars. https://www.tribegroup.co/ is a marketplace app which connects social influencers with businesses for this purpose.

For app entrepreneurs with limited funding, there are more creative ways.

Ask them

Simply ask your targeted celebrities and influencers to use your product and spread the word if they like it. Message them via social media or go to places and events where you can meet them. Become their client if they offer any services. Focus on building relationships with their close associations, like personal assistants, PR managers, hairdressers, and personal trainers. Get those people to use your product and introduce you and your app to the celebrity. Give them free access before the product is even publicly launched. Educate them on how your app would help their fans and followers.

Find a common cause/purpose

Many celebrities are passionate about a social cause. They believe in some higher purpose. Does your app's purpose align with theirs? Even if your app doesn't directly contribute to a specific social cause or a purpose, you can associate yourself with a charity or non-profit. For example, you may decide to contribute a certain percentage of your profits to educating kids in underdeveloped countries. Then you can identify and approach celebrities who are already involved in some charities that improve the conditions of kids in underdeveloped countries. Businesses can be a force for good. With this approach, you can not only grow faster but also do some good in the world and feel a greater sense of fulfilment.

Work out a deal

Instead of upfront payment, offer a small equity in your business or royalty in your product sales in exchange for endorsing your app. Even better, ask them if they would like to invest in your app and promote it. Stamped, an app for reviewing businesses and restaurants, has investors like Ellen DeGeneres, Ryan Seacrest, and Justin Bieber. Justin Bieber also took an equity stake in Shots, a selfie-sharing app for which he led a $1,100,000 seed round. Shots' popularity spiked when Bieber started using it to post his own photos: http://blog.hollywoodbranded.com/celebrity-investments-blog-post

Many other celebrities, like Leonardo DiCaprio, Jay Z, Ashton Kutcher, Tom Hanks, and Jessica Alba have invested into tech startups. It's certainly a trend for celebrities to get involved in the tech space, and many are inspired and looking for good opportunities.

Don't procrastinate. Be bold.

Before you approach celebrities, you must fully believe in yourself and your product. Many people self-sabotage by procrastinating. They find excuses, like "My app is not looking good enough yet; it's not working 100%; if I lose them, I lose them forever," etc. Start approaching the right people now even if you think your app is not fully ready. Tell them you are almost ready and use the meeting to share your passion and gauge their interest. Don't procrastinate.

25. How to promote your app by standing on the shoulders of the giants

Along with App Store optimisation, advertising, and celebrity endorsement, another powerful way to grow your app business is to strategically partner with established brands. This method is probably the one that can give you the highest return on investment.

Partnering with big companies is proving to be a very effective, efficient method for startups to acquire users. It's not David versus Goliath; it's David befriending Goliath. Building a strategic partnership allows you to leverage millions of dollars and years of work a corporation has put into their own marketing to help you promote your product. It creates a mutually beneficial business relationship.

Choosing a strategic partner

There are four basic elements to look for when considering a strategic partner.

Similar target market

Look for companies that serve the same market as yours. For example, let's say your app targets young parents. Think about partnering with toy companies or local child care centres.

Shared values

You can start a partnership with any company if you hustle. But for the partnership to be successful in the long term, you need to partner with a company that has similar values. For example, if you value people over profits and your partner values profit over people, it's not going to be long before the partnership faces challenges.

Common mission

If you partner with someone who has a similar mission, it will be much easier to get things going in the right direction. For example, Alibaba's mission is to make it easy to do business anywhere. Jack Ma, founder of Alibaba, said company mission is the first thing he looks for when partnering with other companies. He only partners with companies which also strive to make it easier to do business.

Value for your partner

Think about which company can leverage the most value from your startup. Value can come from any number of factors, but assuming you are a tech/app startup, often your product can offer unique technology. Target companies who can offer additional value to their customers using your technology.

Examples of strategic partnership between app startups and big brands

- One great example of strategic partnership is online music app Spotify. It partnered with Adidas to create the Adidas Go app, which uses Spotify's extensive library to play music according to the pace and intensity of the user's workout. The partnership provided unique technology for Adidas, and access to hundreds of thousands of Adidas customers for Spotify.
- Uber is the king of partnership. In its early days, Uber partnered with different event companies running big conferences and expos in major cities. Uber would offer conference participants a discount code to use Uber, and get the event companies to send emails to thousands of their visitors about the offer from Uber. Uber worked with Google to put Uber on Google Maps when users

search for their destination. This partnership put Uber in front of millions of new users. Launched November 30, 2012 in Australia, Uber exceeded the one-million user mark in Australia by 2016.

- Buzzfeed, an app that provides personalised news to users, partnered with GroupM, one of the world's largest distributors of online ads. GroupM provided significant advertising for Buzzfeed in exchange for access to Buzzfeed's unique Pound technology, which provides user analytic data of how stories spread on the social web.

- Hipstamatic, a photography startup, partnered with Instagram to integrate the two apps so users take and edit photos in Hipstamatic and then push them to Instagram with one tap. These photos when posted on Instagram have a "Taken with Hipstamatic" tag that links to the Hipstamatic website. Because of this integration, Hipstamatic gained exposure to millions of Instagram users. Instagram CEO and cofounder Kevin Systrom said, "Really, it all comes down to this: people post Hipstamatic photos on Instagram all the time, and we just want to make that experience easier."

- Unidesk provides software to deploy Windows apps. It partnered with Dell, and Dell included the software as part of its solution offering in Desktop Virtualisation Solutions. Unidesk's unique technology added value to Dell's existing customers; Unidesk gained access to Dell's millions of customers.

- So, who are your potential targets for a strategic partnership? What do you have to offer? How will you benefit?

Once you make a "hit list" of companies, identify people in those companies. LinkedIn is probably the best tool to research, identify, and contact senior people in big companies. With the LinkedIn premium plan, you can email people outside your network. Be a great networker. Go to events and conferences where people from your hit list of companies might attend. Introduce yourself and offer to buy a coffee. Share with them your app idea and the partnership opportunity, ask them who would be the right person to talk to about this partnership. Work your way in.

26. How to turn your users into your marketing team

The most successful apps are the ones that spread like virus. They leverage their existing users to spread the app to new users, using techniques like viral marketing, viral loops, and the network effect.

What is viral marketing?

The concept of "viral marketing" was first popularised by Hotmail in 1995, when they put "Get your free web-based email at Hotmail" in the footer of every user's email. As a result, they added 270,000 new users every single day. In December, 1997, Sabeer Bhatia sold the service to Microsoft for $400 million.

The key distinction of viral marketing is its compound effect. Traditional marketing follows the shape of a funnel, channelling from more users to fewer users. For example, one thousand users see your ad, one hundred click the ad, and one downloads the app. But viral marketing follows the shape of an inverted funnel, working from few to many users.

One user downloads the app, he/she invites 10 users, those 10 users invite 10 users each, and the funnel gets wider and wider.

Viral marketing is a phenomenon in which people actively spread a product or service to others, either voluntarily or involuntarily. In the Hotmail example, it was involuntary; users spread the service just by using it. Viral marketing can also be created artificially, by creating an incentive for a user to invite other users.

Create viral loops

Some of the world's greatest apps have been built with incentives for their users to invite more users. For example, Dropbox offers free storage if you invite a friend to create a Dropbox account and they do so. Uber gives taxi credit when you share your experience with your friends and invite them to use the service. Airbnb offers hosts travel credit for introducing new hosts to Airbnb.

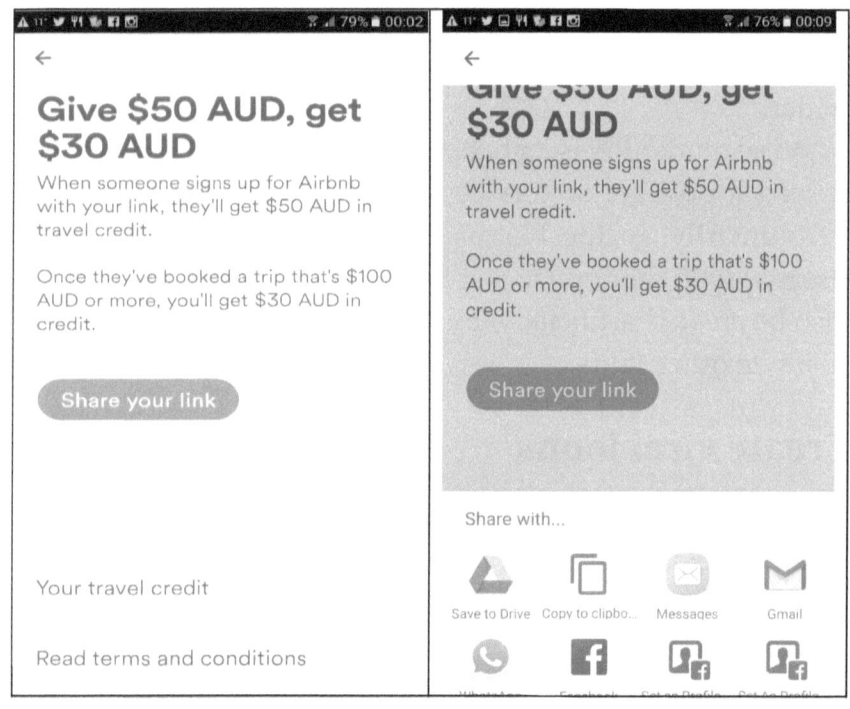

Image: AirBnB creates viral loops by offering travel credits to its users.

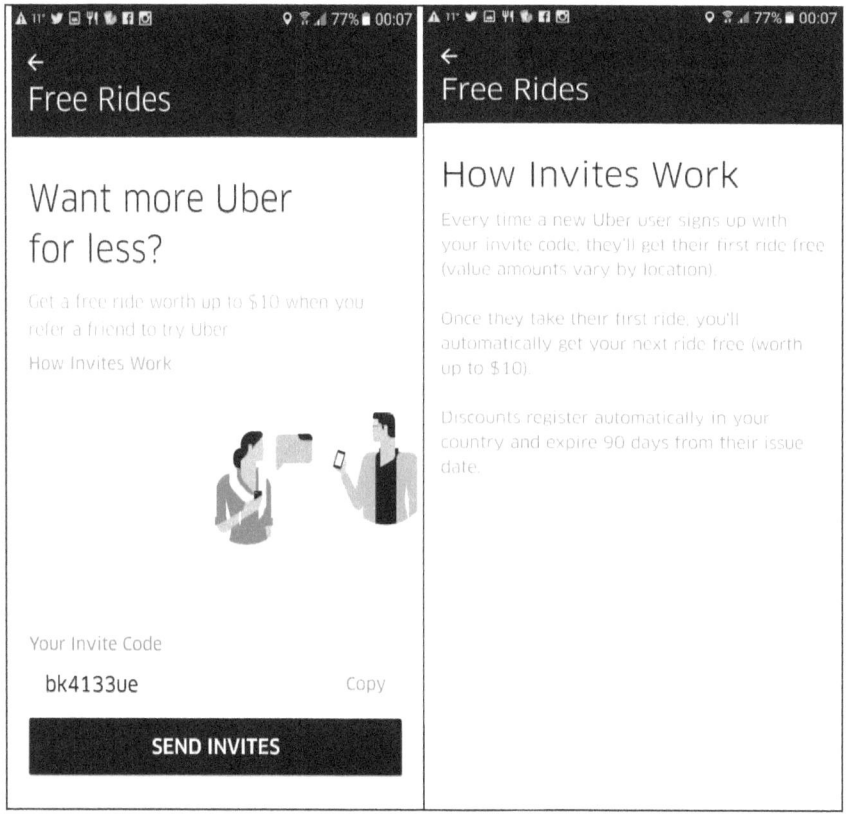

Image: Uber creates viral loops by offering taxi credit to its users.

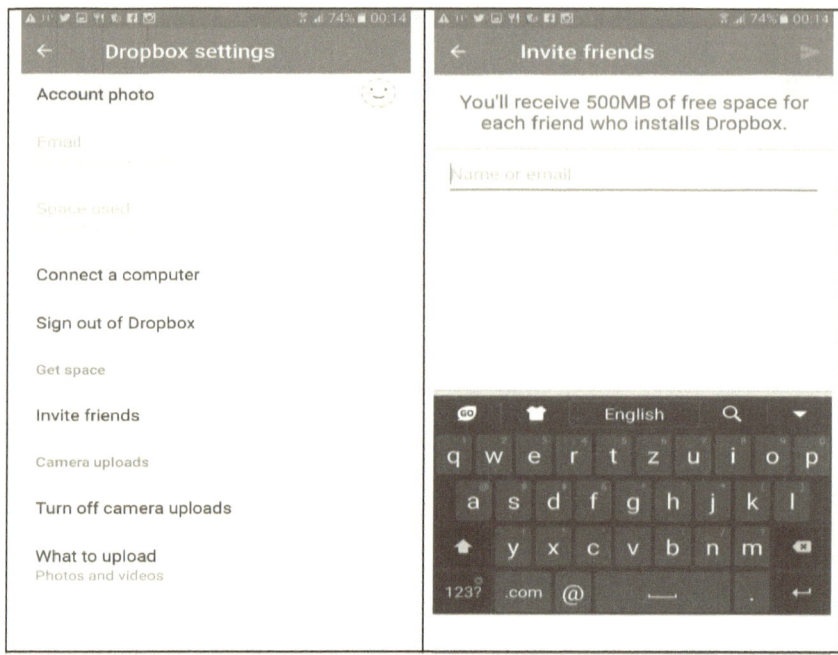

Image: Dropbox creates viral loops by offering free storage to its users.

What feature can you build into your app to create this viral loop? This is a very hot topic in app marketing, and you can find plenty of books, articles, and websites on this topic if you Google "viral loops."

Build network effect

The *network effect* is a phenomenon in which a product becomes more valuable and useful when more people use it. Facebook is a great example: you love it even more when all your friends are there participating with you. WhatsApp is more useful when all your friends and family use it, as it makes communication quicker and easier. With the WhatsApp app, you can invite all your phone contacts to download/use the app.

The network effect motivates users to invite their contacts to use an app because it will make the app even more valuable for them, and because it's fun to share. Does your app make use of the network effect? Does it have a feature that makes the app more valuable to a user when their friends, family, and colleagues use it as well?

Keep in mind that all of this works only when your product is great. Viral loops and the network effect are just two possibilities for successful marketing that will add to your success and position you to produce that *next* great app idea that's rattling around in your brain.

Alicia Redman
★☆☆☆☆ 23/12/2016

Doesn't work anymore.
I loved this app, but now randomly all my snap chats fail to send. I can usually load friends' chats and see what they are up to, but I can rarely respond. I will rate higher if someone could tell me how to fix it. I've Uninstalled, updated, and reinstalled the app several times. No luck so far.

Jack Brinegar
★☆☆☆☆ 23/12/2016

Broken
This is literally the worst performing app I have ever used. It's so slow that whenever I see that it updated I come here to re-give it one star

Rowdy Guy
★★☆☆☆ 23/12/2016

Discover is trash
Please for the love of god allow topic selection for Discover. The absolute last

Salih Oman
★ ☆ ☆ ☆ ☆   23/12/2016

Just stop
There are way too many updates. And
good job this new update I already saw two
big bugs good job. Now the videos freeze
before they end god more problems

yolan d
★ ☆ ☆ ☆ ☆   23/12/2016

Memories 😿
What the hell Snapchat Team!!! I lost
some really nice pictures because of your
memories feature. Looks like there are
multiple bugs with it. You guys should have
kept save to memories and camera roll as
default to avoid all this hassle. Not a well
planned update xxx

Bianca Rodriguez
★ ☆ ☆ ☆ ☆   23/12/2016

Freezes up constantly
It doesn't back up or save any of my stories
properly! I lost precious vacation videos in

Allie M.
★★☆☆☆ 23/12/2016

Needs to be fixed ASAP!!!
I have a Samsung Note 4 and SNAPCHAT keeps crashing. Every time I take a picture using face recognition it crashes!!! This needs to be fixed before I give it more stars. Pretty sad that the app works with Apple phones perfectly fine but sucks with Samsung... COME ON!!!! *12/23/16 UPDATE!* Problem still hasn't been fixed!!! Now it's even worse. It now sucks my battery to no end, it shuts my phone down AND to top it all off it STILL crashes!!! Please fix this SNAPCHAT!!!

Dotty Woods
★★☆☆☆ 23/12/2016

crashing?!?!
After I send about 3 or 4 snaps or I watch a snapchat story... the app freezes and crashes... sometimes causing my entire phone to crash... this has only started happening after the last few updates but i

SECTION 7: WHAT IS INVOLVED IN MAINTAINING MY APP?

27. Why apps need maintenance

Many app entrepreneurs assume that their work is finished when the app goes live. After having the idea, finding the money to help bring it to life, polishing all the bugs out of it, and getting it live on app platforms, the work is far from over, and a different stage of the journey begins.

Once your app is live, it is living in an environment of users, devices, and operating systems which constantly change. There are three main reasons you must maintain your app to keep it alive:

- Whether your app is iOS or Android, device specifications like screen size, resolution, and operating systems are always changing. You must update your app so it stays compatible and works as expected.
- Feedback from your users will alert you to new scenarios, ideas, and bugs that you never knew existed.
- Regular app improvements are critical to stay relevant in the market. They allow you to communicate with your users, motivating them to be active in your app instead of competing apps.

As an example, let's look at the Windows operating system. Windows 1.01 was first launched in November of 1985, but

Microsoft has released new versions every year since then. The software is still not 100% bug free. It crashes, it gets hacked, people love it and hate it—and after all that, it's the highest-revenue-producing software ever in the history of software sales. Microsoft is still working on it, and will always be working on it, because nothing stays constant in the software ecosystem.

"But that's Windows," you protest. "That's the basis of the majority of operating systems all over the world." So, let's consider some specific apps.

If you go to Facebook's app page in the Play Store, you'll see they update the app every week, fixing bugs and improving performance. You'll also see hundreds of negative reviews: the app is too slow, doesn't open, crashes, takes too much space, etc. The same is true for many apps; take a look at the user reviews page for Snapchat.

Even multibillion-dollar companies like Facebook and Snapchat, employing hundreds of the world's best software engineers, can't create bug-free apps. But the good news is that the bugs, crashes, and bad customer reviews did not stop them from becoming multibillion dollar apps. It should not stop you either.

There are just too many variables in the software environment, including:

- Operating systems and their evolution
- Device capabilities (processor speed, RAM, storage, screen size and resolution, integration factors, etc.)
- Devices themselves: phones, tablets, watches; what's next?

It's also the nature of software development. The more complex the app is, the more things that can go wrong. With time, with more users and more data, the apps grows continually more complex. Apps with millions of users have a team of site reliability engineers whose job is only to make sure the site/app is available without interruption.

Aside from the technical environment, the market also changes. New compliance requirements are introduced. Competitors introduce cool new features, and you need to match or exceed them. Users request new functionality and contribute fun ideas.

In short, maintenance is required for however long you want your app to stay usable and relevant in the market. But that's good news! It keeps your app active and profitable, and it builds a community just waiting for your next app to be released.

You can do a number of things to keep maintenance hassle-free and under your control. In this chapter, you will exactly learn that.

28. Keeping app maintenance under control

There are four main areas to set up and use that will help you keep maintenance under your control, instead of the other way around. They are:

- Documentation
- Proactive testing
- Source code version control
- Support system

We'll look at each in turn.

Documentation

This is a process to start early in your build process. You document your app features and functions in a requirement document. You also document information and make comments within your source code, so anyone can understand the code quickly. Good developers maintain proper documentation that pays dividends for the lifespan of your app. Every time you make changes to the app, you must change the documentation to reflect it or at least update your documents every three to six months.

For instance, what happens as team members come and go? It's almost certain that different people will work on your app over time. Good documentation saves hundreds of hours of time in analysing, understanding, and explaining the app to new team members.

Proactive testing

Before you go live, you will test your app using a variety of popular devices and operating systems. But as the environment in which the app lives constantly changes, you never stop testing. Regular proactive testing ensures you find issues before your users do. This will allow you to prevent negative reviews on your App Store page.

You'll test your app, not only to see that it works as you intend, but also to see what happens under heavy usage. This is referred to as load testing. Is there enough memory in your server? If the usage increases by 1000% overnight, will it crash? Load testing is done by creating an artificial load (instead of real users) on your app and servers by using software tools. This allows you to prevent the app and app server from going down when usage spikes unexpectedly.

Source code version control

As the developers work on your app's code, they have different versions of the code which relate to different versions of your app. Your developer should maintain each version with information on what part of code is changed, added, or removed, and why. Without it, things can get messy. For example, say the new version of your app includes a camera integration feature. If this feature update is affecting the performance of other parts of your app, you may decide to go back to the previous version. Source code repository tools allow you to do that easily by maintaining source code versions effectively. There are many free and paid tools, based on features they offer.

BitBucket and GitHub and are very popular in the app startup community. You can search online for a variety of options.

Support system

Before you go live, make sure you have a great support system in place. This is the foundation of providing good support to your users, as well as maintenance to your app. Support systems (also called issue tracking or ticketing systems) allow you to record and maintain the status (open, in-progress, resolved, or closed) of every issue that arises in your app. All your maintenance tasks, like bug fixing, performance improvements, user experience improvements, and new features, can all be maintained in one place.

There are plenty of systems available. Atlassian's Jira and Freshdesk are really good for this purpose. You can see a comparison of a number of options here.

Maintaining your app can become a wild octopus. Setting up the processes and tools we've reviewed here will let you tame the beast before it unleashes havoc on your app.

29. Support system guidelines

To ensure support systems are useful, you need to use them correctly. Let's take a closer look at the process involved as maintenance issues arise, are tracked, and get resolved in the support system. What I share here is just a method and there are a number of methods and steps you can use for this purpose. There are five main steps to tracking issues in a support system:

- Logging
- Categorise and prioritise
- Fix
- Test
- Deploy

Logging the issue

When someone spots a problem, they create a "ticket" to log the issue and start the process. Tickets can come from your own team, while testing the app, or, after launch, from end users' feedback, and are recorded in the issue support software.

In fact, you can even allow your users to log issues directly into your support system. You've probably experienced this if you've ever emailed a support request on a software company's website and received an email in return giving you a reference number for your ticket. Many support systems, like Freshdesk, allow your users to report issues directly from within your app, and logs them automatically to your support system. At this stage, the status of the issue is marked "Open."

Categorise and prioritise

Once a ticket is logged, the support team analyses and categorises it. Maintenance tickets can be classified into three main categories.

- Functional issues. A feature in your app is not working as expected. Examples include "User is not receiving notification," or "User is not able to flip camera from back to front when they tap the relevant button."
- Performance issues. For example, the app opens too slowly, freezes, crashes, or logs users out. Performance is a moving target; speed or other performance markers may be acceptable now, but expectations a year from now may change significantly. Proper maintenance keeps your app performing up to user expectations.
- App enhancements. Good maintenance includes regular updates. Adding features based on user requests and market research keeps users engaged.

After categorisation, each ticket is prioritised according to the severity of the issue. The commonly used terms are *critical*, *major*, and *minor*.

- Critical issues are those which stop the user from using the application: crashes (app closes automatically and exits the user out of the app), freezes (app becomes unresponsive to all interactions), servers/websites going down, etc.
- Major issues are caused when main features of the app do not perform as expected. Issues that recur frequently may also be considered major.
- Minor issues could be simple UI glitches or problems with less important features of the app. Issues that occur very occasionally may also be seen as minor.

- At this stage, when your support team is working on an issue, they change the status of the issue from "Open" to "In progress."

Fix and test

Once tickets are prioritised, the developers have an order in which to address them. They fix the problem, test their fix, and submit it for User Acceptance Testing. The team may change the status of the ticket to "Fixed" or "Pending approval." Only after the product owner or typical users test the app and say the problem is fixed is the issue considered resolved and marked "Resolved."

Deploy

Now the fix is deployed to the App Store or Google Play in an app update. The ticket status is marked as "Fixed-deployed" in your issue support system. If the same issue occurs again, you can also Reopen an issue that was Closed or Resolved.

Now the stages and the words used for the status are just examples. Different systems use different words. The key is to have a system and a process so any one in your team including your users can know the status of a ticket by simply logging into the system. Without such a system and process in place, maintaining a live app can become very challenging.

30. Other essential tools for effective maintenance

There are a few other tools involved in the maintenance process that deserve our attention.

Test environment and test build distribution software

As you maintain your app, you need a place where you can run new versions of your app safely and test them before putting it live. A test environment maintains a duplicate of your entire app infrastructure, but is exclusive to your team and not accessible by the public. This is where changes are made and tested before being deployed live.

For web apps, you can simply create a duplicate of your web app in a separate server instance that is not public but known only to your team.

For iOS and Android apps, there are tools to help you distribute and manage test builds effectively without putting them out on app stores for public view. TestFlight is a popular test build distribution software which was recently bought out by Apple.

HockeyApp and BirdFlight are also popular tools used for this purpose.

Crash analytics

This is software that tracks app crash information for you: when did your app crash, under what scenario, in which devices, in what operating system, etc. Gathering this kind of data without using a crash analytics software can annoy your users. Without such analytics in place, it would require asking each frustrated user who experienced a problem with your app to supply their mobile device details. Instead, you can track it automatically by integrating crash analytics tools in your app.

Crashlytics is the most popular crash reporting app.

Count.ly and Applause also offer crash tracking, along with many other features.

User Analytics

There are many analytics tools that allow you to gather data about your app and your users. With app analytics tools in place, you can focus on the features that are most used, and ignore features that aren't.

For instance, when Burbn (now Instagram) found that none of their users were using the check-in feature, but they all seemed to love the photo-sharing feature, they used that information to dictate their direction. They focused only on photo sharing (Instagram) … and that seemed to work out pretty well for them.

Analytics can help you decide which features you should or should not be building, fixing, and optimising.

Analytics tools can provide heaps of useful information about your app and your users, for example, the devices and OS of your users, their location, how many hours per day they use your app, how long they use the app in one session, when the last time they used the app was, etc., that will help you make important business decisions.

Mixpanel, Flurry, and AppsFlyer are some of the popular app analytics tools available in the market.

As you can see, launching your app is only the beginning. App support is a major area of ongoing effort in creating a successful app business. You can do it effectively by using the right tools and by building the structure for it from the start.

31. User driven development

From the many conferences I have been to and from spending time with a lot of successful marketers and entrepreneurs in Silicon Valley, if I had to pick one thing common among the most successful apps, it would be how much focus they put on the users' feedback after they go live.

A survey was conducted in a growth marketing conference (December 2016) in San Jose to find the average time it took for the successful startups among the participants to go from idea to a successful app. The finding was that it took an average of 12 to 24 months to go from idea to live and another 12 to 24 months to go from live to having a product that customers love and can be scaled with a repeatable sales/marketing model (product-market fit).

It is the 12 to 24 months after going live that contributed most to the success of these apps. Most of the successful app companies ran user feedback sessions with their app users on a weekly or fortnightly basis. Some even talked to their users daily. They incorporated the user feedback into the app immediately, making the users their loyal brand advocates.

Net Promoter Score (NPS) is one of the key metrics all the successful app companies focus on. The NPS question is "On a scale of 1 to 10, how likely are you to recommend the app to your friends, family and colleagues?" Users who score from 1 to 6 are your detractors, 7 to 8 are indifferent about your app—passives—and those who respond with 9 to 10 are your promoters or brand advocates. Your goal is to get the majority of your users to be your promoters, i.e. score 9 to 10 for the NPS question.

How quickly you can execute valuable user feedback into your app determines how quickly you can improve your NPS. So running good user feedback sessions and having the systems and process in place to execute the user feedback is a key part of the ongoing maintenance to make your app successful.

User feedback can be gathered using a number of different formats like online survey forms, one-on-one interviews, and focus groups. Ideally you need to use a combination of all the formats and choose the right format based on the type of feedback you are asking for. For example, online surveys are good for a quick quantitative survey about the app, one-on-one is good for getting specific user experience feedback on a new feature you are building, and a focus group is good to discuss broad topics/ideas to decide what new features to build in the app. Go to appomate.com.au/resources to download templates with sample group discussion questions, app feedback questionnaires, and one-on-one interview questions to help you gather valuable feedback from your users and target market.

SECTION 8: LIVE BIGGER!

32. End game: living bigger

The potential of your app business is limited only by you. That is why we started the book focusing on you.

Throughout this book, you learned the key steps involved in living bigger.

11. Know your "why" and what kind of app business you want to create

12. Pick a great idea that solves a significant problem

13. Validate it. Don't assume your idea is great. Test your assumptions as quickly as you can

14. Fund, build, and grow it

15. Live bigger

The key is to acknowledge that it's not the idea, but it's often the entrepreneur who creates legacies. Remember this: "If you (and your team) cannot execute the idea better than anyone else can, then you don't deserve to win big."

Always work on yourself. Build on the skills and knowledge you need to become a successful app entrepreneur. Build a great team around you. If one idea fails, pivot to the next one, persevere, and you are surely on your way to living bigger.

I hope you enjoyed the book. This book is only a small step in going from an idea to having a successful app. But success is often made of a thousand small steps, not one big jump. So congratulations, you are one step ahead. If you are determined to be successful as an app entrepreneur, if you feel the need to have someone keep you accountable and want to be part of a community of app entrepreneurs, check out Appomate.com.au/appmastermind. I am giving away a limited number of free three-month memberships to my App Master Mind program.

Congratulations on completing this book. You now have a great understanding of how to create an app and grow rich. I encourage you to continue to refer back to the ideas and resources in this book as you continue to learn and grow. I wish you all the best in your app entrepreneurship journey.

Live Bigger,

B Kris

ACKNOWLEDGEMENTS

A very special thank you to my business partner, Tim Moon, for his support in so many different ways. He guided me throughout my business journey not only as a business partner but as a mentor, an investor, and more than anything, a friend and a brother. I thank him for allowing me to stay in his beautiful holiday house where I spent days writing this book. Above everything, he helped me understand the power of being trusting and trustworthy. He encouraged me to start this book, finish this book, and also contributed to section one of the book. Thank you, Tim.

Thanks to my wonderful colleagues and teammates, Vishwas Prasad, Kevin Chin, Dan Boyce, Gengarajan, Nandhakumar, Anumothu, Ramamoorthy, every one of you for your hard work in helping our clients while I had my time away from the business working on many fun things, including this book. Thanks to all my clients/business partners/friends, Nick Liolios, Shane O'Neill, Steven Farrugia, Cassandra and Adriaan Hall, Adrian Di Natale, Ron Van Der Schalk, Geoff Roosen, Brad Joneic, Patrick Marion, Billy Cooper, Ann Austin, and many others for trusting me and my team with your big app ideas. Thank you.

I also thank my entrepreneurial friends, Jack Delosa, Andrew Morello, Petar Lackovic, Tim Morris from The Entourage, Jeffrey Slayter and Kane Minkus, Dr. Louise Mahler, and many others who have been a huge inspiration for me to always learn, lead, and live the dream.

And last but not the least, I thank my parents who have supported me in all the decisions I have made. My dad taught me the power of patience and being grounded and my mother showed me the joy in helping and educating others.

Special thanks to Mary Beth who helped me proof read/ edit the book and Dave Thompson for helping publish the book and make it a bestseller.

ABOUT THE AUTHOR:

B Kris (Barath Krishnamoorthy) is the founder and managing director of Appomate, an Australian app company. B moved to Australia in July 2008 as a student/immigrant from India, founded his business in December 2011, and took the business to seven-figure revenue and six-figure profits in less than five years. His company apps are used by staff and customers of enterprises like Hoyts, Lend Lease, Groove Train, Adidas, and L'Oréal.

Among B's highest values are freedom and fun, and his vision is to inspire and enable more freedom, fun, and growth in people's lives. Like everything else he does, he believes his business, Appomate, will contribute to his vision by creating brilliant, world-class app products and app entrepreneurs.

Outside his app business, B spends his time in personal development workshops, meditating, dancing, yoga, festivals, travelling, snowboarding, reading books, training/coaching people, doing nothing, and all things that help him grow, have fun, and feel free.

You can find out more about his company at Appomate.com.au and read his blogs at bkris.com

Your Special Gift For Buying This Book:

I want to personally thank you and congratulate you for getting this book. As a gift, I would like to give you a FREE 3-month membership to my "App MasterMind" program.

This program includes:

- Access to a monthly webinar discussing various topics on app entrepreneurship
- Q & A with Barath following the webinar
- Become part of our community of app entrepreneurs
- Access to an online education portal.

To claim your gift, go to Appomate.com.au/appmastermind.

References

http://thenextweb.com/dd/2013/12/02/much-cost-build-worlds-hottest-startups/#gref

http://investor.fb.com/releasedetail.cfm?ReleaseID=908022

http://www.rewardleholdings.com/annual-reports/

https://www.stock-analysis-on.net/NASDAQ/Company/Facebook-Inc/Financial-Statement/Income-Statement/Quarterly-Data

https://investors.atlassian.com/financials-and-filings/financial-statements/default.aspx

http://www.payscale.com/research/IN/Job=Senior_Web_Developer/Salary/4ae7f1cb/Mid-Career

http://www.payscale.com/research/IN/Job=iOS_Developer/Salary

https://www.glassdoor.co.in/Salaries/ios-developer-salary-SRCH_KO0,13.htm

http://www.timesjobs.com/jobskill/Junior-Ios-Developer-jobs

http://www.scmwise.com/software-engineering-salaries-india.html

www.ingramcontent.com/pod-product-compliance
Lightning Source LLC
Chambersburg PA
CBHW021951170526
45157CB00003B/938